NOV 2 8 1989	DATE DUE	
2		

THE APARTHEID CRISIS

OTHER BOOKS BY OLIVER WILLIAMS:

Full Value: Cases in Christian Business Ethics
with John Houck

The Judeo-Christian Vision and the Modern Corporation
edited with John Houck

Co-Creation and Capitalism: John Paul II's Laborem Exercens
edited with John Houck

*Catholic Social Teaching and the U.S. Economy: Working Papers
for a Bishops' Pastoral*
edited with John Houck

THE
APARTHEID
CRISIS

How We Can Do Justice
in a Land of Violence

Oliver F. Williams

PERENNIAL LIBRARY

Harper & Row, Publishers, San Francisco

Cambridge, Hagerstown, New York, Philadelphia, Washington
London, Mexico City, São Paulo, Singapore, Sydney

FIRST EDITION

Library of Congress Cataloging-in-Publication Data

Williams, Oliver F.
  The apartheid crisis.

  Includes index.
  1. Investments, American—South Africa. 2. Corporations, American—South Africa. 3. Apartheid—South Africa. 4. Race relations—Religious aspects—Christianity. 5. South Africa—Race relations.
I. Title
HG5851.A3W55 1986   332.6'7373'068   85-45726
ISBN 0-06-250951-9 (pbk)

88 89 90 MPC 10 9 8 7 6 5 4 3 2

For my mother and father

CONTENTS

ACKNOWLEDGMENTS

I am indebted to many people and institutions for assistance in this project. The Rockefeller Foundation and the University of Notre Dame generously funded travel and research time for the study. My colleagues, John Houck, Lee Tavis, Ronald Morris, David Schlaver, C.S.C., Edward Malloy, C.S.C., Roger Crawford and Dennis McCann offered suggestions for the manuscript. The last chapter was presented at the 1986 Annual Meeting of the Society of Christian Ethics and I owe much to the helpful comments of my friends. I am grateful for the support and encouragement of Frank K. Reilly, Dean of the College of Business Administration and Rev. Theodore M. Hesburgh, C.S.C., President, University of Notre Dame.

During the summer of 1985, I spent four weeks criss-crossing South Africa observing the scene and interviewing almost a hundred people. Archbishop Denis Hurley, my host in Durban, South Africa, during the research phase in July 1985, deserves special mention. His insight into the great tragedy of South Africa is only exceeded by his genuine love of people—*all* people. I hope that some of that spirit comes through these pages.

Oliver F. Williams, C.S.C.
University of Notre Dame
May 1, 1986

INTRODUCTION

The apartheid laws of South Africa are offensive to most Americans. These racial laws deny blacks the right to vote, to move freely in their own country to attend the (better) white schools, and to own businesses in white communities. There is a growing movement in the United States to force the over 280 American firms who run operations in South Africa to leave the troubled nation. This campaign has a number of strategies, the most popular being divestment, that is, the selling of stock of institutions that have operations in South Africa. Over ten states and thirty cities have passed laws restricting or forbidding investment of public monies, including pension funds, in firms involved in South Africa. University endowments are under increasing pressure to make similar rulings. The hope of some advocates is that divestment will eventually cause U.S. firms to leave South Africa (disinvest), which, in turn, will either pressure the white rulers to change their racist policies or will create a climate for revolutionary action. Others argue for divestment and disinvestment from the principle of avoiding complicity in evil, while a third group is primarily concerned to show solidarity with the oppressed by prophetic activity.

Individual stockholders as well as institutions are being asked to take a stand on the question of investments in South Africa. For those persons and institutions who are avowedly Christian, the issue is more pressing. How does one translate the biblical injunction "to love one's neighbor" into this difficult and complex arena? This challenge is the concern of the pages that follow. The book outlines the problem in South Africa, its history, the various strategies proposed for solution and the relevant biblical and theological themes. It then argues for continuing U.S. investment under certain conditions.

Chapter 1 opens with the story of a young black manager in South Africa, one of those few lucky ones who work for a U.S. multinational. The story shows his suffering as a result of laws that institutionalize racism, laws such as the pass laws, influx control, and the Group Areas Act. He struggles to raise a family and lead a normal life. This narrative is followed by the story of a white executive, portraying his typical day. The contrast demonstrates that skin color is *the* factor that determines level of affluence and life-style in South Africa. The reader comes to see how difficult it will be to vanquish the horrible monster called *apartheid*. On the other hand, there are some grounds for hope in the fact that since this chapter was written, President P.W. Botha announced that the hated pass laws would not be enforced as of April 1986 and would soon be abolished. If this move actually allows blacks to live and work where they choose, it is a major step.

Understanding the history of apartheid is essential. The majority of South African whites are of Dutch heritage and date back to the settlements of 1652. These people call themselves "Afrikaners," and they consider South Africa their home. Although today the white population constitutes only one-sixth of the total (5 million out of 32 million), they continue to exercise almost all power in the nation. In Chapter 2, I review the religious, political, economic, and cultural history of these whites and blacks, and explain how the present state of affairs arose.

Key actors presently advocate a number of strategies to overcome apartheid. In Chapter 3, I review the highlights of these proposals and offer some interpretation of them. First, I consider the South African government's position, and then outline programs of the opposition party, the African National Congress, the United Democratic Front, Inkatha, the South African Council of Churches, trade unions, and the South African business community. After briefly considering the long involvement of the United Nations, I conclude the chapter by considering the major actors within the United States: the Reagan administration, the Free South Africa Movement, and the business community. I also examine the role of the Sullivan Principles in the U.S. debate.

In the final chapter I argue that the appropriate Christian response to U.S. investments in South Africa is a synthesis of religious commitment with political and economic judgment. Although many contend that the biblical witness to avoid evil precludes investing in an apartheid regime, this presentation takes a wider view of the biblical witness. A biblical standpoint must be informed, not only by Jesus' avoidance of evil but also by the reality of sin and the vocation to work for a just world. In this light, if it can be shown that the political and economic welfare of blacks will be enhanced by foreign investments in South Africa, then these investments are moral. Although I admit the plurality of Chirstian vocations, and thus the important role of prophetic witness against the evil of apartheid, I argue that the stewardship ethic—using corporate power to advance black welfare—holds the most promise at this juncture. To realize this promise, however, the business community must begin dramatic new initiatives that clearly show everyone that they are listening to the blacks of South Africa.

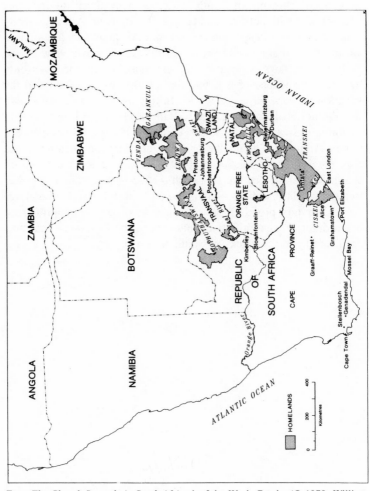

From *The Church Struggle in South Africa* by John W. de Gruchy (© 1979, William B. Eerdmans Publishing Co.). Used by permission.

Chapter 1

TWO DIFFERENT WORLDS: A BLACK PERSPECTIVE

Moses Mpunthe, Robert Foley, Simon Middleton III and Buti Matshitsi
are composites created for illustrative purposes and are not actual people.

Moses Mpunthe switched off the alarm and shifted his attention to the hands of the clock: 6:30. Time to begin another day. Life in Soweto was complicated these days, what with the state of emergency and all. South Africa had not had a state of emergency for over fifteen years, and Moses wondered how long this one would last. On 21 July 1985, State President P. W. Botha had declared a state of emergency for some of the most densely populated black townships. For ten months, life in these black areas was marked by continual protests against apartheid, and the white police now had been granted new powers to maintain white control: to search homes, seize property, detain people without charges, and ban meetings. Almost six hundred people had lost their lives in the violence, many killed by police; Moses hoped some good would nevertheless come of all this grief.

Moses plugged in the electric coffee pot. Electricity, taken for granted now in most homes in Soweto, had opened up a whole new world for the township. When Moses was growing up, he had to study by candlelight or lantern. Now modern lighting and even street lighting ran throughout the town. Moses sat a moment, considering the momentous changes in Soweto since his childhood. As a junior executive in a large U.S. pharmaceutical firm in Johannesburg, he now appreciated his schoolteacher mother, who had drilled him in academic subjects at home after school hours, and who had imbued him with the discipline and ambition to go on to college. He was one of the few of his generation in Soweto to continue his studies. In fact, although much had changed in Soweto, it was still a bleak, despair-ridden place.

Moses was proud of his four-room house, which marked him as a member of the middle class in the township, although there were larger houses than his. The standard house was a 9- by 12-foot, boxlike structure with a corrugated metal or fiber roof. Built of dull buff bricks on small plots of leased land, the houses are almost always on dusty unpaved roads; only the main arteries in Soweto are paved. Under a new dispensation from the government, Moses was recently able to purchase his house. What a joy that was! To actually own a house in the white man's land! Up till then, blacks were able to own a house only in the so-called homelands, the 13 percent of the country set aside exclusively for blacks. In fact, Moses knew only too well that it was just recently that the law allowed him to own the land on which his house was built, for until a year ago blacks could only get a 99-year leasehold on their land in Soweto.

The "homelands." What a joke! Moses knew that more anger and frustration centered on the notion of "homelands" than any other in the world of blacks. One of the predecessors of P. W. Botha, Hendrik Verwoerd, had drafted a system whereby every black was assigned to one of ten homelands on the basis of tribal ancestry. Thus, for example, a Zulu was assigned citizenship in Kwazulu, an assortment of land parcels in the province of Natal on the eastern seaboard of South Africa. Even though the person might never have been in his homeland, or even live there during his entire life, he would still have citizenship there and thus would have no claim to citizenship in white South Africa. The ten homelands were carved across the country in areas that were often dry and barren. At present, about half of the 23 million blacks live in one of the homelands, while the remainder live in one of the black townships that form satellites around all the white towns and cities. Verwoerd's eventual goal was to have all ten homelands independent, and thus have South Africa for whites only. To be sure, blacks would still be living in black townships outside white cities, for blacks were needed for industry and domestic service, but they would be "guests" only, not citizens.

This bit of game playing could be very painful for those classified as "citizens" of homelands that had become "independent nations." Although no nation in the world will recognize them as such, South Africa considers four homelands as independent: Transkei, Bophuthatswana, Venda, and the Ciskei. Moses knew several friends in Soweto who were classified as Tswanas and thus were considered citizens of Bophuthatswana. When Bophuthatswana was declared independent, all Tswanas in black townships lost their citizenship in South Africa. Although they are allowed to remain in Soweto for their lifetime, their children are classified as foreign blacks and must return to Bophuthatswana at age sixteen unless they are fortunate enough to obtain jobs and permission to remain in the township. The worry and anxiety this problem has caused for parents is legend. State President P. W. Botha has repeatedly promised that citizenship would be restored to all black South Africans, but it is unclear what he means and when he intends to do it.

The 3.5 million blacks who have been forcibly removed from "blackspots" (black communities in so-called white areas) and resettled in the homelands have suffered intensely. Moses thought of a friend of his, Smangaliso, who drove a truck in Johannesburg. Even though he himself had a proper pass to work, his wife and children were almost a hundred miles away in a homeland. Smangaliso lived in a hostel for men only and, if he was lucky, he saw his wife and family on weekends. Few job opportunities existed in the homeland, and most able-bodied men tried to get to the cities for employment.

Getting to the cities, however, was becoming more and more difficult for blacks in the homelands. All blacks had to carry pass books (or reference books) at all times when outside of the homelands. In April 1986, P. W. Botha announced that the pass laws would no longer be enforced. It is still unclear if blacks will have freedom of movement. The book included work history, prior residences, present permission to live in a "white area," and indication that taxes have been paid. Through the reference book system, "influx control officials" have unsuccessfully attempted to ensure that the number of blacks allowed out of the homelands was no more and no less than the number required to keep white South Africa efficient and comfortable. Moses remembered, from his college days, a sentence often quoted by his favorite professor, from a

1922 study by the Stallard Commission: "It should be a recognized principle that Natives—men, women and children—should only be permitted within municipal areas in so far and for so long as their presence is demanded by the wants of the white population."[1] Those words were etched on Moses' soul, for he knew that they were still the guiding vision of the government of South Africa. Moses could feel his anger welling up as he pondered the plight of his many friends arrested for pass law violations. In recent years, millions had been arrested and charged under the 1952 law. The state president often had promised to repeal the influx control laws, but nothing had been done.

Enough daydreaming. Moses picked up his attaché case, quietly closed the door, and faced the chilly July weather. Soweto is over a mile high, and early morning temperatures are in the 40s (Fahrenheit) in the winter months of June and July. He breathed in the acrid air; a haze permeated as far as the eye could see from the thousands of coal stoves in the township. He could almost taste the sulfur in the air. Opening the door to his two-year-old Toyota, he smiled wryly to himself. Here he was, driving a company car, making a good salary in a management position where he supervised over 50 people, including ten whites, and yet he was living in a ghetto. True, it was one of the more affluent black townships in all of South Africa, but it was still a ghetto.

The official population of Soweto was listed at about a million, but anyone living there knew it was more like 2 million, for illegals were everywhere. Each morning over 400,000 blacks left their homes in Soweto and made the three- to four-mile trip to Johannesburg for a day of work. Although the middle class was growing, most blacks were just eking out a living, and many lived in overcrowded slum conditions where crime thrived and family life had little support. Moses felt great satisfaction knowing that he had made it to the top (for his people), but he knew that things were much different for his thirteen-year-old son. His son was angry, for he wanted a future, and Soweto looked bleak, no matter how much "whitey" tried to spruce it up.

As he drove through the dusty side streets to the asphalt main road, Moses passed dozens of people making their way to the buses or trains that would carry them to Johannesburg. In recent years, some were even grouping together and sharing a fare in the ever-expanding taxi business of Soweto. You could tell when you were approaching Johannesburg, for curbs and sidewalks began to appear. Who ever dreamed twenty years ago that there would be a traffic jam on a road from Soweto? It was true blacks had come a long way—but then again, they still had so far to go!

Johannesburg was a land of skyscrapers, new cars, and bustling crowds of people. Moses had visited corporate headquarters in New York last year, and the closest parallel to Johannesburg he had seen was lower Manhattan. He parked his car in the company garage, got in the elevator, and pressed the button for floor 20. He knew he would shortly feel like a new man, someone important, respected for his competence regardless of what color his skin might be. He had to admit, he really enjoyed work, though he did feel guilty at times that so many of his black friends could not share his temporary liberation.

Awaiting him on his desk was a memo indicating that there had been a work stoppage in one of the company's plants on the outskirts of town. Although this was not his direct area of responsibility, he was asked to help, since the incident involved a racial problem with the blue-collar workers. Of course he would help. He went immediately to the office of the industrial relations officer for a briefing. It turned out to be the sort of incident that occasionally occurred these days. While waiting in a cafeteria line, a white had accused a black of stepping on his foot. The black denied it and was slugged by the white. The black labor union called for immediate discipline of the white worker, who happened to be an assistant foreman in one of the shops. Union rules called for a due-process procedure that normally took two to three days but the blacks did not trust management and declared that they would not work until the ruling had been handed down. Management tried to assure the black workers that justice would be done, but the workers would have none of it.

Moses knew the problem. The blacks had few civil or political rights, and they were seething with anger over their second-class status. Unions were the one place where they had a hand in shaping their own destiny, and they reacted to every infringement of their rights like a recoiling spring. Moses would meet with the black leaders and assure them that the investigation and penalties would be fair. He knew that they would hear him out, but he knew as well that they probably would not return to work until the white man was disciplined. They had had enough. Moses understood.

It was not too long ago, Moses recalled, that blacks were not able to have unions. Now the workplace was the most democratic place in white South Africa. Most U.S. and U.K. companies were in the vanguard of this movement, largely through the efforts of Rev. Leon H. Sullivan. Sullivan, a black pastor in Philadelphia and a member of the board of directors of the General Motors Corporation, called twelve major U.S. companies together in 1977 and drew up a code of conduct that has come to be known as the Sullivan Principles.

Moses knew the code well, for one of his roles in the company was to monitor its implementation: (1) nonsegregation of the races in all eating, comfort and work facilities; (2) equal and fair employment practices for all employees; (3) equal pay for all employees doing equal or comparable work for the same period of time; (4) initiation and development of training programs that will prepare blacks, coloreds, and Asians in substantial numbers for supervisory, administrative, clerical, and technical jobs; (5) increasing the number of blacks, coloreds, and Asians in management and supervisory positions; and (6) improving the quality of employees' lives outside the work environment in such areas as housing, transportation, schooling, recreation, and health facilities. Within the workplace, the code had long since been standard policy and Moses knew that his own life was much more pleasant because of it. Outside the workplace, land was still zoned by skin color and over 300 laws enforced apartheid, the Afrikaans word for "separate development" (literally "separate-hood"). In 1985, Rev. Sullivan and the now 128 signature companies added a new requirement to the code: all U.S. companies operating in South Africa would "support the ending of all apartheid laws."

Moses could still remember the exhilaration he felt when he heard that his company would actively lobby the South African government to end apartheid laws. The lobbying for the most part, was to be done through the American Chamber of Commerce (AM-CHAM), an industry-wide association of all the U.S. firms in South Africa, and Moses was assigned as a member of the steering committee. The AMCHAM committee prepared a hard-hitting document that placed industry squarely in opposition to the apartheid laws. The position paper covered urbanization and influx control, housing, removals, migrant labor, black business rights, and citizenship. It also argued for channels for democratic participation at all levels of government, the means of which were to be arrived at by negotiation and consultation with all leaders of the various constituencies. The final document was officially presented to a special Republic of South Africa (RSA) cabinet committee and it was widely publicized. Moses had never worked so hard on a project in his whole life. So much was at stake. He had waited so long, and he knew he would have yet a long wait before he and his family tasted real freedom. He had little confidence in the white South African government and knew that the blacks were in for a long power struggle.

Moses caught himself daydreaming again, and brought his mind back to the day's work. In twenty minutes he had an appointment with Robert Foley, a senior vice-president from corporate headquarters in New York. The New York office normally would not give such attention to the relatively small operation in South Africa, but in recent months the pressure by activists for U.S. disinvestment had made South Africa a major concern for all top management. Moses knew that the home office feared activists would call for a boycott of the company's product in the United States until the company closed the South African plants. The present corporate strategy was to continue to publicize in the United States all that the company was doing in the Republic of South Africa to overcome apartheid, in the hope that activists would be persuaded to stop short of boycotts or demands for disinvestment. Rob Foley was in town to get an update of the company's initiatives for blacks. Moses had given his briefing to so many VIPs from "the States" in the last few months that he knew it by heart. The major items flashed before his mind:

1. *Programs designed to eliminate apartheid in the workplace.* Here principles one to five of the Sullivan Principles are discussed.
2. *Programs designed to improve the quality of employees' lives outside the work environment (Principle Six).* Here Moses

would describe how the company funds technical training centers where thousands of blacks learn essential job skills. He would also describe Pace Commercial College, a first-class five-year school in Soweto, which boasts the finest facilities of any black township. Scholarships are available for highly qualified applicants, and the school prepares students for university courses as well as for business careers. U.S. companies initiated the project and continue to sustain it. The company also participates in the Adopt-a-School program, in which management time and cash grants are made to a select number of schools in black townships, to enhance and improve the educational process.

3. *Programs designed to lobby in South Africa for the elimination of apartheid.* Here Moses would tell of a new initiative by American corporations called the U.S. Corporate Council on South Africa. The council was comprised of the chief executive officers (CEO) of the major U.S. firms operating in South Africa. One of Moses' tasks was to make suggestions to his CEO in New York as to the most effective ways the council might address the RSA government. He was currently working on some proposals that went beyond the American Chamber of Commerce statement made in the spring of 1985.

The secretary buzzed, and Moses knew that would be Rob Foley. He looked forward to the meeting, for Rob was the sort of person you felt comfortable with. A former college athlete, Rob was smart as a whip, but a gentle guy who always tried to make everyone look good. Moses went to the door and greeted Rob warmly. In short order, Moses was well into the briefing with Rob giving him his undivided attention. Moses could tell that Rob was worried about the company in RSA.

After three hours of briefing and intense discussion, Rob interrupted Moses to say, "Let's go to lunch. I saw a nice place down the street while walking here from my hotel." Moses knew the place; it was one of the favorite watering holes for executives in the Market Street area. He also knew that as a black, he was not welcome. This was Rob's first trip to South Africa and now was as good a time as any to start educating him about the reality of apartheid. Moses explained that the restaurants that have a "Right of Admission Reserved" sign displayed usually are not willing to serve blacks. Other restaurants without the sign may or may not. The only sure restaurants for blacks looking to dine in a "white area" are "international" restaurants. He suggested the dining room at the Carlton Hotel, one of the finest in Johannesburg, and off they went.

Moses explained that some of the hotels, especially the newer, more expensive ones, went to the government and insisted that blacks be able to reserve rooms and use the bar and dining facilities. Hotels wishing to cross the color line were then designated "international." The Carlton was one of the best in Johannesburg, and Moses knew that few, if any, blacks from Soweto would ever stay there, but it did provide first-class service for blacks on business from the United States. Moses always felt good about ordering at the Carlton, and he knew the black waiters enjoyed serving the rare black brother who wandered in.

Rob was dismayed to find how much segregation was still present in a "progressive" city such as Johannesburg. He thought "petty apartheid"—segregation in restaurants, hotels, parks, buses, and so on—had been eliminated. Moses assured him that he was wrong. Trains and buses were segregated. In many cities dual bus systems for whites and blacks were marked with clever signs to indicate which is which. In Johannesburg, white bus stops were announced by a white sign with black letters saying "Bus Stop," while the black bus stops were marked by a black background and white letters. So that blacks would not sit on benches at a white bus stop, there was a sign saying "Bus Passengers Only." Since the black bus stop was generally several blocks away, apartheid was enforced without ever calling it to the attention of visitors. Moses went on to tell Rob that almost all beaches were still segregated, and many movie theaters as well.

After a leisurely lunch and long discussion over how much was yet to be done before blacks could feel at home in their own country, Moses suggested that they adjourn and return to the office. He suspected that Rob was shaken, for he seemed to be distracted. On returning to the office, Moses learned from his secretary that his wife had called to say that there was unrest in Soweto that day. The children in a number of schools in the black township had refused to return to the classrooms after lunch and were on a rampage. Moses's young son was among them. Moses worried about his son. He was not as angry as many of the neighbors' children, but he was clearly caught up in the fight.

Black high-school students were highly organized in an activist group called the Congress of South African Students (COSAS), and although COSAS was now outlawed, it was still very alive. Moses knew that the black student unrest all across South Africa was not merely coincidental, but the fruit of a highly disciplined group of angry young people who were determined to destroy the "system." The boy living across the street from Moses was a leader in the movement, and he frightened Moses. He called his peers "Comrade" and talked of the wonders of Marxism and the evils of capitalism. It saddened Moses because it was clear that the youth, like many others, had identified the whole apartheid system with capitalism and had therefore passionately supported its antithesis, Marxism. In fact, the students knew very little about either of these "isms."

Although there had been earlier disturbances in Soweto in 1976 and 1977, the uprisings in black townships that began in September 1984 had taken on a ferocity heretofore unknown in South Africa. Clashes with police and military took place almost every day, and the intensity of conflict was alarming. Moses had listened to his son and his son's friends and knew their complaints by heart: the inferior education for blacks provided by the government; the promise of reform of apartheid with little or no substantial action; the difficulty for black youths in finding jobs; the rising prices of housing, rent, and bus fares; the insulting move that gave colored (mixed race) and Indians representation in a tricameral parliament yet excluded blacks; the corruption and ineptitude of local leadership; and the feeling that no matter how hard they worked they still had no future—at best, they would get a house in a ghetto and be treated as fourth rate by the white rulers. It was quite a list of grievances, and Moses knew they were all true. What really worried him was the small number of young blacks who had no agenda other than to destroy. The cry of some of Soweto's youngsters had become *Siyayinyova*—"We shall destroy." They had grown impatient with the pacifism and impotence of their parents' generation and the ineffectiveness of their leaders. They burned, looted, and resorted to violence because they rejected everything and everybody; this spirit of anarchy that could finally destroy all that Moses had always worked for—a country where blacks and whites could live and work together as equals.

Moses quickly phoned his wife. Although they had waited almost two years before the government telephone service could install their phone, it was worth the wait. His wife related the scope of the troubles. The unrest was fairly widespread, so the police had sealed off Soweto. That had not been difficult, because all black townships were deliberately laid out with few entrances and exits. A buffer zone lay between beautiful Johannesburg and bleak Soweto so that in serious trouble troops could be staged. Bus and train service had been suspended to avoid damage from rocks and gasoline bombs, the weapons of the blacks.

Moses would sleep in the office this night, for there was little chance of getting home safely. He was anxious for his son. The police were getting tired, and violence was almost inevitable in these confrontations. First the police would use tear gas and rubber bullets. Tear gas was sprayed from machines mounted on Land Rovers; these ''sneeze machines'' were becoming commonplace in Soweto. If the people would not disperse before these weapons, the police would often charge swinging flexible whips about a yard long called *sjamboks* (pronounced ''SHAM-bocks''). If the whips did not work, usually they resorted to birdshot from twelve-gauge shotguns. Finally, there were real bullets, shot from rifles. The police moved around the township, from disturbance to disturbance, in heavy armored trucks nicknamed ''hippos.'' If they were lucky, Bishop Tutu, the people's great hero, would come on the scene and try to calm the restive crowds.

Moses sat at his desk, and he prayed. He prayed for his son, that he might be safe; his wife, that she might always be at his side; for all his friends in Soweto that they might find some peace and dignity. Tears began to well up in his eyes, and he cried. He cried like a baby. He had worked so hard in everything he did, and all he could bring his family were tear gas and *sjamboks*. He really did not know how long he could go on.

A White Perspective

Simon Middleton settled back in his easy chair after a hard day at the bank and sipped his brandy. It was nearly 8:30, and the news soon would be coming on the television. Tonight was Tuesday, so it would be in English. What a damnable idea, he thought, alternating the language on television each day between Afrikaans and English. In Middleton's view, television news was the low point of the South African day. Owned and operated by the government, the news was carefully edited so as to put the RSA government in the best light. Middleton often thought that if he were ever driven to drink, it would be because of the frustration of watching the terrible news programs on television.

He was grateful that tonight, at least, he would not have to hear it in Afrikaans. Visitors from the Netherlands could make out what was being said in this hybrid language so treasured by the Dutch-German whites in South Africa, but most Americans found it unintelligible. The initial development of Afrikaans came from a corruption of the Dutch language by the early settlers from Europe (German and French Huguenot extraction), the local Khoikhoi, as well as Malay-Portuguese from the Far East. Later influence came from the 1820 English settlers and the other local Bantu languages. Although Afrikaans was spoken informally, it was not the official language of the land until the twentieth century.

Major progress towards recognition came in the late nineteenth century with translation of the Bible into Afrikaans. A guiding light was Dominee (Rev.) S. J. du Toit (1847-1911) who is regarded as the soul and leader of the language movement. He did not live to see full and final recognition of the language by Act of Parliament in 1925.

The national anthem "Die Stem van Suid-Afrika" (The Voice of South Africa) is in Afrikaans, and its words "Ons sal Lewe, Ons sal Sterwe, Ons vir Jou, Suid-Afrika" (We shall Live, We shall Die, We for Thee, South Africa) embody the indomitable spirit of the Afrikaner. Their language, along with their separate schools and churches, and their great love of the land—these were everything to many Afrikaners. Middleton never could understand the mentality of this breed, and what he did understand he did not care for.

Simon Middleton III was his full name. His grandfather had come to South Africa from the United Kingdom to work for a major Johannesburg mining company. Simon's father was a banker in "Joburg," and he had followed in his father's footsteps. After studying at the University of Witwatersrand, he went to England for graduate work at the London School of Economics. Now in his early forties, Simon was an officer in a major South African bank. Given his education and his family connections, his fast track career was not surprising for South Africa. In fact, the problem was that there were not enough people with the managerial expertise to run the nation's commerce. The skilled worker shortage was even more acute. With black unemployment well above 25 percent, it was embarrassing to explain to foreign visitors that the reason more blacks were not in managerial and skilled labor positions was that, as a matter of government policy, few blacks were provided an adequate education.

Simon knew his interpretation of events and policies in South Africa was biased, for he just could never get himself to like Afrikaners. More fairly, he could never quite see the world from their point of view. About 60 percent of the 5 million whites call themselves Afrikaners, and most of these are descendants of the Dutch, German, and French settlers that arrived in the mid-seventeenth century. When Simon spoke of the Afrikaners, he actually meant the large majority of this ethnic group that bonded together in the Nationalist Party and who have been controlling the government since winning the 1948 elections. A key element of the Nationalist Party platform in 1948 was separation between the races, *apartheid*. Education, travel, work, and living space would all, by law, be separate. In that way the white race could survive, the Nationalists argued. More often the platform was couched in terms that spoke of full opportunities of development for all the races, but everyone knew what was meant. It certainly was separate development but it clearly was not equal development.

Simon reflected on some of the stark contrasts between RSA whites and blacks, from statistics he had just read that very day:

	WHITES	BLACKS
Life expectancy	70 years	57.5 years
Average annual earnings for workers	$8,260	$1,815
Government per capita expenditures on education	$780	$110
Average monthly pension payments	$94	$41

Simon recalled a lunch he had recently with the owner of one of the leading firms that constructed swimming pools. The man claimed that over a quarter of a million white homes in South Africa had swimming pools, a fact that Simon did not find surprising. He knew that most of his friends had black servants and yard boys; it was estimated that almost one million blacks worked for whites in some domestic capacity. Most whites in the RSA had a lifestyle considerably higher than the typical U.S. white.

Now the news came on—there it was, the lead story that Simon was waiting for: Finance Minister Barend du Plessis was announcing that all South African companies were forbidden to repay loans negotiated from foreign banks. Given the way it was reported, Simon knew, most people would not understand the depth of the crisis. As a banker, he knew that, at least temporarily, the whole South African economy was in deep trouble. For bankers, the last eight weeks had been a nightmare; it all had culminated with the finance minister announcing that the South African private sector would default on about $10 billion of debt that fell due within the year. Although the government knew such drastic action would risk cutting off credit for the future, there was really little choice.

How had it all happened? Although Simon had analyzed the sequence of events any number of times and understood what had happened, he still could not believe that it had actually occurred. South Africa had a strong economy with a solid trade position and a sound government treasury. Yet major banks from Britain, Japan, Switzerland, West Germany, and the United States had refused to renew loans to South Africa. Called "rolling over," this process of renewing short-term loans had heretofore been automatic. South Africa was considered to be a safe, secure investment—to the point that foreign banks had invested an estimated $24 billion in the nation. Now, all of a sudden, South Africa was considered a risk. The reason: continued racial violence. Simon sipped his drink and sadly reflected on the dilemma of the land he loved. How could the country move out of the cul-de-sac it was in now?

Although Simon knew that the international bankers would soon work out a plan for rescheduling the country's foreign debt, he could not foresee a happy ending to the country's racial violence. In the long term, the country's future depended on racial harmony and that would only come when the blacks were treated as equals, having all the political and civil rights the whites now enjoyed. Would that day ever come to South Africa? Simon hoped and prayed that it would, but he was at a loss to see how it would happen in the near term.

The problem was in the numbers: whites were outnumbered by blacks almost by a factor of six. The whites had tried all kinds of schemes to maintain all the power—the homelands, white job reservation, restrictions of black businesses, and so on—and for a while these policies had worked. The strategy of the white ruling class was to do anything that would hinder the emergence of a unified black political group. The name of the game was survival, and the Afrikaners played it well. Now, however, the nation was at a crossroads. The blacks were increasingly agitating for political and economic rights, to the point of disrupting the whole economy. Could the whites broaden the democratic processes to include blacks without losing all that whites had ever worked for? Simon thought that most Afrikaners assumed they could not.

In Simon's view, Afrikaners' self-understanding was essentially that of the dominant group, most of them could not even conceive of a South Africa they did not control. He knew he was being harsh, and certainly he had Afrikaner friends who took quite another view of the matter, but Simon believed that most Afrikaners saw recent events as a pure power struggle, a struggle they were determined not to lose. Simon had to admit, at times he had some sympathy for the Afrikaner position. When the day comes that blacks are treated as equals whites would suffer tangible losses, not only in political power but also in real income. Taxes would be higher, and black competition in business would erode the white monopoly power that presently prevails. Simon wondered: Perhaps, that is why, unconsciously, I have never actively sought to put my convictions on black equality into practice. Things are muddled. At least he had always contributed funds to the Black Sash, the organization of English-speaking women who actively work for constitutional rights of blacks.

Simon remembered the words of his father when the new Progressive Party first challenged the then traditional, but now defunct, Official Opposition United Party of the late General Jan Christiaan Smuts. He had sarcastically observed that many of his contemporaries "had talked Progressive, voted U.P., and hoped like hell that the Nats weren't voted out of power!" The Progressive Federal Party, under the leadership of such people as Colin Eglin and Dr. van Zyl Slabbert, had now in fact become the Official Opposition Party.

Things certainly *were* muddled. Simon remembered how surprised he was when one of South Africa's most outspoken and famous religious leaders had told him privately at a dinner party that under no circumstances could blacks run South Africa today. What he meant was that blacks, largely because of white policies that denied them access to the better schools, did not possess the managerial skills to run a government as sophisticated as the RSA government. Many white South Africans also remembered with alarm the post-colonial events in territories to the North—the resultant vacuum of acumen after English, Belgian, Portuguese, and French rule; the excesses and corruption of power; the genocide; the threat of Marxism—the exchange of one tyranny for another. Even the new neighboring state of Zimbabwe did not seem to some to be doing much better under Mugabe than it did under Smith. To be sure, there was a growing number of blacks moving into important managerial roles, especially in business, but many more were needed. To run the country blacks would need political and social institutions to form consensus and develop a vision for the nation. All this was far from a reality.

Simon knew that in his own banking corporation hundreds of blacks had been brought in, trained, and promoted in the last ten years. They even had several black vice presidents and there were plans to hire additional ones. Hiring blacks made good business sense as well as moral sense. Blacks at present have more than 50 percent of the RSA consumer power, and this figure is likely to expand rapidly in the coming years. The business community had been making a concerted effort to hire and train blacks for important roles and the major business and trade associations have been quite candid in asserting their belief that free enterprise could be a major engine of political reform. In 1978, when P. W. Botha came to power, the *verligte* (enlightened) Afrikaners heralded a new day when substantive reform would become a reality. Simon still remembered the famous 1979 meeting in Johannesburg when Botha met with the leaders of the business community (largely English speaking South Africans) and spoke of the great role of business in overcoming apartheid. He meant what he said, apparently, for his state budgets reflected a 50 percent increase in allocations for black training.

Six years later, however, the now State President Botha (his title and role were changed with the new constitution in 1984) still had not made any substantive reforms in "grand apartheid"—that whole web of laws that denies citizenship and free movement to blacks. Repeatedly, Botha spoke of reforming the pass laws, and citizenship of some sort, but there was no follow-through. Like any politician, Botha had his finger held up to test the wind and the 1981 elections saw 15 percent of his Nationalist Party defect to the conservative alternative, the Herstigte Nasionale Party (HNP). Although they did not win any seats, Botha was chastened in his reform agenda. The party for most liberal Afrikaans and English-speakers was the Progressive Federal Party (PFP) and they captured 19 percent of the vote in the last election.

To Botha's credit, he had finally repealed the Immorality and Mixed Marriages Act, allowing sexual relations and marriages across the color bar. For blacks, this meant absolutely nothing, although Simon felt the repeal undermined the conceptual foundations of the whole system of race classification. Simon recognized that blacks, struggling for some semblance of dignity, had little time for discussions of conceptual foundations, and so was not surprised when blacks almost ignored the latest concession of their white keepers. As a history buff, Simon read the history of the United States with interest. He admired Abraham Lincoln. Simon thought of his own nation and the crying need for a man of great vision and character. He was saddened, for he recognized that while the country needed an Abraham Lincoln, it had a Richard Nixon.

In fact, many in Botha's Nationalist Party were antigrowth and this stance troubled Simon. Unlike most businesspeople, such conservatives saw economic expansion as undesirable, for it would bring more and more blacks into relatively affluent situations in the white cities. Political rights would be the next step. This advance, of course, was precisely the dream of many like Simon Middleton, but probably the "Nats" would stifle it, if they could.

Simon noticed that the news was over. He finished his drink, and got up to take a walk around the yard.

As he strolled through the back lawn, the moon illuminating the property, Simon thought how lucky he was to have been born white. He had a beautiful twelve-room home surrounded by well-kept lawns and carefully tended gardens. The Middletons had two garden boys working at the place, and although he knew they really did not need that many, the setup did, he thought, help alleviate the chronic black unemployment problem. The swimming pool needed daily cleaning, and that took one of them the whole morning. He and his wife each had a Mercedes, and the cars needed washing at least twice a week. With these boys and the cook and the maid in the house, Simon knew that he had more help than any of his counterparts in England or America would dream of having. But South Africa was different. Simon selected garden boys who wanted to learn a trade, and he paid for their part-time education. Over the years many had gone on to be quite successful in one or another skilled job. It was the least he could do, Simon thought. With the whole staff at the house, the total cost of salaries came to less than $300 a month.

Simon reflected on the terrible plight of the blacks who were newly emerging into the middle class of Johannesburg. One of the black vice-presidents, Buti Matshitsi, had come in to talk to him that afternoon and shared some of his heartache. Although relatively affluent, Buti had to live in Soweto, for all land in South Africa was zoned by race. Simon's white friends often spoke as if the RSA were now a meritocracy, but they seemed to forget that the meritocracy only existed in the context of a racial hierarchy.

Buti could not forget it, for he had to apologize continually to his black friends for being co-opted into the white man's world. He told Simon that he always took off his suit jacket and tie before driving back through the streets of Soweto, for fear that some young radicals might accost him. Buti trusted Simon and he had shared some thoughts that had severely shaken Middleton. Buti was considering leaving the bank and joining the outlawed African National Congress (ANC). He would go to Lusaka, Zambia, the external headquarters of the exiled movement, and serve in a senior leadership position. Simon knew that most young blacks considered the ANC their only hope, and many were leaving the townships to train in terrorist tactics with the ANC in Zambia and other nearby nations. He could not believe that Buti would even think of leaving the bank for the ANC.

Simon rehearsed his thoughts, which he planned to share with Buti the next day. There was cause for hope that blacks would get full rights in their native land of South Africa. Since 1979 blacks have been able to form trade unions, and today over fifty black unions are registered with the government, and many more are actively representing their members. With the right to strike and raise money, blacks are getting a taste of freedom—there will be no return to the old days. Even more, he thought, the business community of South Africa was the most progressive institution in the country and repeatedly issued strong statements urging the government to negotiate with the whole spectrum of black leaders a new political future for blacks.

The four major business organizations of RSA, including leading Afrikaans and English-speaking executives, had closed ranks in arguing for the need for urgent reform in the nation. U.S. corporations, through the American Chamber of Commerce in RSA and the U.S. Corporate Council on South Africa, had applied great pressure on the Afrikaner government, and there was a good chance of significant reforms in the near future. Simon realized, of course, that the business leaders were making every effort to distance themselves from the government. They had given up on behind-the-scenes lobbying and were openly critical, in hopes that even if the government would not change, at least they would have the continued loyalty of their black employees. This support they needed for survival.

An important sign of hope for the future was that young Afrikaans-speaking students were beginning to speak out about the need to reform. In the last year the president of the Afrikaanse Studentbond (ASB) issued a statement that called for the scrapping of influx control and for negotiation on other issues of critical interest. Simon put great stock in this trend, for these sons and daughters of influential Afrikaners would soon be running the government. Also, the recent repeal of the Prohibition of Political Interference Act, now allowed nonracially separated political parties. Although the ruling Nationalist Party had made no attempt to include all races, the Progressive Federal Party had an aggressive drive underway to recruit coloreds and Indians. To be sure, blacks did not have the vote, but the tide had turned. It was only a matter of time, in Simon's view. Multiracial political parties were a sign that living together in harmony was a possibility.

On the other hand, Simon could understand why Buti would think of joining forces with the ANC. Simon wondered for a moment—if he were black, might he also be tempted to join a group that planned to overthrow the white oppressors? Certainly many whites were themselves troubled about the injustices in the land. Figures from the Central Statistical Services in Pretoria showed that there was a tremendous "brain drain" in South Africa—over a thousand professionals per month were emigrating to Britain, Australia, and other more peaceful countries. Conscription, which is required of all RSA white males for two years, had increasingly become a problem as whites were forced to battle blacks in their own land. Over 7,000 white males evaded the draft last year after the army had been used to patrol violence in the black townships. This increase was dramatic, and Simon expected the number to rise even higher as the use of army troops in the townships increased. As he thought about his meeting with Buti the next day, he grew sadder and sadder. Maybe he should *encourage* his black friend to go to Zambia.

NOTES

1. For a discussion of this principle of the Stallard Commission, see Mere Lipton, *Capitalism and Apartheid* (Totowa, New Jersey: Littlefield, Adams & Company, 1985), pp. 18, 22, and 139.

CHRONOLOGY OF EVENTS

1486 Bartholomew Diaz of Portugal circumnavigates Cape of Good Hope

1497 Vasco da Gama sails around Cape of Good Hope on the way to the Indies.

1602 Dutch East India Company is formed.

1652 Jan van Riebeeck arrives at Cape to set up a half-way station for Dutch East India Company.

1657 A small group from Dutch East India Company is allowed to farm on Cape.

1665 First Dutch Reformed Minister arrives.

1688 French Huguenots arrive.

1786 Missionary work among slaves and Khoikhoi is begun.

1795 Cape is occupied by the British.

1803 Cape Colony is returned to Batavian Republic.

1806 The British occupy Cape Colony.

1820 Thousands of immigrants from England arrive.

1833 Slavery is abolished.

1835 Great Trek begins.

1838 (16 December) Victory of Blood River is achieved under Andries Pretorius.

1839 White members of Dutch Reformed Church (DRC) in eastern Cape ask for separate communion: not granted.

1843 British occupy Natal.

1848 British occupy Orange River Sovereignty.

1853 Representative government is established in Cape Town.

1854 English give Trekkers the Republic of Orange Free State.

1857 Synod of DRC reluctantly allows separate communion and separate services.

1868 Diamonds are discovered at Kimberley.

1870 Anglicans found Church of the Province in South Africa (CPSA).

1871 Britain annexes the diamond fields.

1877 Britain annexes the Transvaal.

1884 Gold discovered on the Witwatersrand.

1897 Sir Alfred Milner becomes British High Commissioner of the Cape Colony.

1899–1902 Anglo-Boer War is waged.

1908–1909 National convention is assembled.

1910 Cape, Orange Free State, Transvaal, and Natal are merged into Union of South Africa.

1911 Mines and Works Act is passed (later amended by the Color Bar Act of 1925).

1912 African National Congress is formed (originally called South African Native National Congress).

1914–1918 World War I is waged.

1923 Native Urban Areas Act passes.

1924 Nationalist Party wins; James Hertzog becomes prime minister.

1925 Afrikaans replaces Dutch as an official language.

1933 United Party is formed.

1936 Representation of Natives Act passes.

1937 Industrial Conciliation Act passes.

1938 Centennial Celebration of the Great Trek.

1939–1945 World War II is waged.

1948 Malan and the Nationalists come to power.

1949 Prohibition of Mixed Marriages Act passes.

1951 Bantu Authorities Act passes.

1952 ANC passive resistance campaign is mounted.
Abolition of Passes and Coordination of Documents Act passes.

1953 Bantu Education Act passes.
Reservation of Separate Amenities Act passes.

1955 Freedom charter is adopted by the ANC.

1958 Nationalist party wins; Prime Minister Verwoerd takes power.

1959 Extension of University Education Act passes.
     Promotion of Bantu Self-government Act passes.
1960 Referendum on Republic status is held.
     ANC demonstrates against pass laws.
     (21 March) Sharpeville Massacre takes place.
1961 South Africa becomes a republic and withdraws from the commonwealth.
1964 Nelson Mandela is sentenced to life imprisonment.
1966 Prime Minister Verwoerd is assassinated: replaced by B. J. Vorster.
1976 Disturbances arise in Soweto and other townships.
1977 Community Councils Act passes.
1978 P. W. Botha succeeds Vorster as prime minister.
1984 New constitution implemented with a three-chamber parliament and a new office of state president (combines previous offices of state president and prime minister).
1985 (21 July) State of emergency is declared in major magisterial districts.
     (August) International banking community refuses to renew loans to RSA.
1986 (23 April) P. W. Botha announces plans to abolish the pass laws.

Chapter 2

A HISTORY OF THE PROBLEM

Love without justice is a Christian impossibility, and can only be prac-
ticed by those who have divorced religion from life, who dismiss a
concern for justice as "politics" and who fear social change much more
than they fear God.

Alan Paton

In viewing the current conflict in South Africa as por-
trayed in the lives of Moses Mpunthe and Simon Middleton, readers
unfamiliar with the national history are bound to be puzzled. How
did such a situation ever develop? Although more oppressive systems exist in the world, apartheid is the only one based on skin
color. Over 300 racial laws deny blacks many of the rights we take
for granted—the right to vote, to move freely in their own country,
to attend the better white schools and to own businesses in white
communities. The history of South Africa could never be condensed
in such a short chapter; my goal here is to provide a brief outline
of the major events that influenced the thinking and shaped the
development of what is known today as the Republic of South
Africa.[1]

Early History

In 1554, a group of Portuguese sailors navigating the Indian Ocean
were shipwrecked on the eastern seacost of South Africa and reported that the people there were "very black in color with woolly
hair." Historians also believe that the Transvaal area was occupied
by black people who moved from the north as early as the fifth
century. Paintings on caves in the Cape area reveal that the brown-
skinned San people (Bushmen) had been living and hunting in the
region centuries before the Europeans arrived in the seventeenth
century. The Khoikhoi or Hottentots, nomadic peoples who tended

stock, shared the Cape region with the bushmen. Although many whites in South Africa still believe that the Africans only later migrated from the north and settled in ''white'' South Africa, little historical evidence supports such an assertion.

The Portuguese, in their quest to reach the Indies, made early history with Bartholomew Diaz rounding the Cape in 1486 and Vasco da Gama sailing along the east coast of the continent in 1497. Shortly after, the Portuguese built a refreshment station at Mozambique, which served ships on their way to the Indies.

The Dutch East India Company located their relief station at the Cape of Good Hope in 1652 when Jan van Riebeeck and 125 men established a colony. Five years later a number of the men were released from the company in order to farm and tend cattle for the station. In 1688 the Dutch East India Company brought some hundred and fifty French Huguenots to the Cape, promising free land for cultivation. Although by order of the Dutch leaders the native Khoikhoi could not be taken as slaves, their grazing and hunting lands were slowly appropriated by the new arrivals from Europe. To augment the meager labor force, slaves were brought in from East and West Africa and from Malaya. Intermarriage between the Dutch and freed slaves was not uncommon in the early days and the resulting population is what is known as the ''Cape Colored'' today. By the late seventeenth century, mixed marriages were officially discouraged, however, so that the mixed-race population is a relatively small group in South Africa today.

The eighteenth-century life in the Cape Colony saw the population rise to almost 15,000 people. Although life was difficult, with ongoing guerrilla warfare with the Khoikhoi and increasing strife with the Xhosa population, the *Trekboers*, as they came to be called, survived with their strong Calvinist faith and their great spirit of self-reliance. They likened their own situation to that of the patriarchs of the Old Testament, facing untold hardships on nothing but their faith in God and their own resources. As the Boers (from the Dutch word for farmers) moved further into the wilderness and expanded their land holdings, life became more dangerous, but these hardy people possessed a passionate conviction that God was on their side. Although the first Dutch Reformed Church (DRC) minister had arrived in 1665, missionary work among the slaves and Khoikhoi was discouraged. The "heathen" could not be baptized, although some exceptions were made in cases where a white person guaranteed the Christian training of a black candidate. Not until 1786 did missionary work become a full-scale ministry.

Early in the nineteenth century (1806), the British took control of the Cape permanently; they had already occupied it briefly from 1795 to 1803. The colony was then a multiracial society with a hierarchical structure of some 22,000 whites and 25,000 nonwhite laborers. To the east were numerous Khoisan and Xhosa. In their push eastward for land, the settlers had repeated conflicts with the Xhosa: in the years 1811, 1819, 1834, and 1836. These skirmishes have become known as the "Kafir Wars." (The word "Kafir" literally means "unbelievers" and today it is a derogatory term. In Afrikaans the term "kaffer-boetie" is the equivalent of "nigger-lover.") In a final act of exasperation, after years of fighting a losing battle, the Xhosa followed an ancient ritual designed to call their ancestors from their graves and to force the whites into the sea. They killed all their own cattle and destroyed their own crops. After the failure of this strategy, almost 30,000 Xhosa traveled west and joined the Cape Colony, while the remainder stayed and perished on their barren land.

Missionary activity increased with the arrival of members of the London Missionary Society and the Wesleyan Methodists. The Methodists made the journey with some 5,000 British immigrants in 1820. This large influx of new arrivals from England added many former city dwellers to the Cape Colony. Increasing missionary activity among the Africans produced a tension still present today. A scholar at the University of Cape Town, John W. de Gruchy, expressed the problem well:

The basic reason that Dutch and English settlers alike resented the presence of some missionaries was thus precisely because the missionaries not only evangelized the indigenous peoples, but took their side in the struggle for justice, rights and land. The missionaries, being white, regarded themselves as the conscience of the settlers and the protectors of the "natives." . . . The church's struggle against racism and injustice in South Africa only really begins in earnest with their witness in the nineteenth century.[2]

The British government took a number of steps to enhance the human dignity of the Africans. In 1828, Ordinance 50 was enacted, which provided for the abolition of passes for Cape Colored servants. The pass was a document required if a servant wished to go out of the assigned residence area. In 1833 slavery was abolished at the Cape. The farmers were enfuriated by these measures, because labor was already exceedingly difficult to control. When, after the 1834 war on the eastern frontier, the British colonial secretary refused to annex the Xhosa land, 4,000 Boers began to move north in what has come to be known as the Great Trek. The Voortrekkers (Pioneers), seeking to escape the British domination, traveled in covered ox-wagons and pushed east across the country to what is today known as the Transvaal.

A seminal event in Boer history occurred when, in February 1838, Piet Retief took a group on a peace mission to the Zulu King Dingaan near Natal. After murdering Retief and his party, Dingaan sent 10,000 men to the main camp of the Voortrekkers and slaughtered the women and children. Determined to get retribution, Andries Pretorius (in whose honor Pretoria, the administrative capital, is named), led the men and sixty-four wagons into Dingaan's area and waited for the Zulu attack. They made a vow that if God would give them victory they would remember the day for all time as a day of thanksgiving. Each evening they circled the wagons to make camp (*laager*) and waited. Finally, on the night of 15 December 1838, the Zulu attacked, and after six hours the Boers emerged victorious, having killed 3,000 warriors. The Ncome River ran red with Zulu blood, and thus the fight was called the Battle of Blood River. Following their vow, on 16 December the Day of the Covenant is a public holiday each year throughout South Africa and Afrikaner citizens give thanks and renew their commitment.

After Blood River, the Boers formed their own republic at Natal, but British annexation of the republic in 1843 forced most of the Afrikaners north to what later became the new Boer republics of the Orange Free State and the Transvaal. These republics too were short-lived. With the discovery of diamonds at Kimberley in 1868, conflict over the land raged. That and the threat of hostile black tribes motivated the British to annex both republics by 1877.

Constant tension crackled between the Boers and the British over how to deal with the race issue. On the one hand, the Boers were not in favor of freeing the slaves. But as John de Gruchy notes, this reluctance stems from deep conviction. De Gruchy quotes a woman who made the Great Trek to escape the British rule:

> Yet it is not their freedom that drove us to such lengths, as their being placed on an equal footing with Christians, contrary to the laws of God and the natural distinction of race and religion, so that it was intolerable for any decent Christian to bow beneath such a yoke; wherefore we withdrew in order to preserve our doctrines in purity.[3]

Whether, in fact, the racial discrimination was subtly based on economic reasons—that is, the need for land and cheap labor that could be met only if slavery endured—is an intriguing question. In any event, the trekker republics were all governed by the principle that the blacks were inferior beings who should live under the unconditional authority of whites. As early as 1839, the white members of a Dutch Reformed congregation in the eastern Cape petitioned to have separate communion based on race. Although their General Synod would not hear of it in 1839 for scriptural reasons, in 1857, acknowledging the weakness of whites who could not accept blacks and coloreds, the synod allowed separate communion and services. The so-called daughter churches for coloreds, Indians, and Africans followed in short order from this separatist policy.

The British colonies of the Cape and Natal took a different tack on relations between blacks and whites. In Natal, the British officer in charge of African Affairs from 1846 to 1875 was Theophilus Shepstone. After Dingaan's defeat, 2,250,000 acres were allocated for the 200,000 Africans who were in need of land. This land was divided into eight reserves and, under Shepstone's guidance, was governed by the hereditary chiefs. In principle, Africans who could meet educational qualifications could vote, but in practice few found their way through the complicated procedure. In 1860 Indians were brought to the sugar plantations of Natal. These laborers had few social and political rights and in the early twentieth century, in the face of this oppression, the famous Mahatma Gandhi first formulated the response of nonviolent resistance. As a British colony, the Cape most clearly reflected the liberal tradition. Afrikaners, British,

Coloreds, and Africans all could vote, although educational restrictions kept the number of Africans who could qualify relatively low.

Scholars have noted that in the nineteenth century, the seminal period in the development of what would become the Republic of South Africa, there were at least two distinct theories of what constitutes an appropriate approach to missionary work with the Africans.[4] One approach argued that tribal life and culture should be infused with Christianity but not merged with white, Western culture. Separateness was thought to be essential to promote and protect the way of life of the African. This theory was congruent with the political vision of those who saw separateness as the only way to ensure the safety of the white communities. Another group advocated the acculturation of blacks into the white communities as the most appropriate way to convert to the Christian way of life. The practice of having separate churches for the races grew to be standard practice not only for the Dutch Reformed Church but also in other Protestant denominations such as the Baptists and the Lutherans. Roman Catholics and Anglicans, on the other hand, in principle could never accept the requirement of separate churches, although in practice the typical congregation was, for the most part, of one skin color.

New-Found Wealth

With the discovery of diamonds at Kimberley in 1868, and gold on the Witwatersrand less than two decades later, South African political and economic life took on a whole new cast. Immigration from Britain increased dramatically, and fortune hunters streamed across the land. In 1871, the diamond area was taken over by the British, and six years later they also annexed the Transvaal. With these moves, the Boers throughout South Africa grew increasingly antagonistic toward the British presence. The antagonism toward a common enemy served to bring together, in spirit if not in physical presence, the widely scattered Dutch-German farmers; it was around this time that they began to call themselves "Afrikaners," a name signifying their unity and common roots. For these men and women, Africa was home.

With the discovery of lucrative gold mines in 1884, the British were intensely interested in controlling the area. After a three-year stalemate between London and Pretoria over conditions for peace in the Transvaal, in 1889 the Boers finally delivered an ultimatum to the British: "Withdraw all troops and submit the dispute to arbitration or we will formally declare war." The rest is history and has become known as the Anglo-Boer War. From October 1899 until 31 May 1902, a painful conflict raged. The Boers lost one-fifth of their population, and many of their women and children were herded into concentration camps. When the British were finally acknowledged as the winner in the 1902 Treaty of Vereeniging, one losing party was, unexpectedly, the blacks. Clause 9 of Article 8 of the Treaty asserted that there was to be "no franchise for the natives until after the introduction of self-government." Colonial Secretary Joseph Chamberlain and Sir Alfred Milner, British High Commissioner to South Africa, in an apparent attempt to appease the Boers, traded off the blacks' right to vote, a right that to this day has never been recognized. Although the Cape kept its nonracial franchise, which provided the vote for over 2,000 Africans and coloreds, this franchise too would be short-lived. Within five years after the end of the Anglo-Boer War, the two defeated republics and the colonies of Natal and the Cape had been granted self-government by the British. In 1910, all four entities—the Orange Free State, the Cape, Natal, and the Transvaal—were merged into the Union of South Africa of the British Empire under an Afrikaner Prime Minister, Louis Botha, who had been a Boer general in the war. The challenge for Botha as Prime Minister (1910–1919), as well as for his successor, Jan Christian Smuts (1919–1924), was to heal the wounds between the Afrikaans- and English-speaking communities and to promote economic growth in the farming and mining industries. The terms of the new union provided that the 1,250,000 whites would have complete political control over the 4,250,000 Africans, the 500,000 coloreds, and the 165,000 Indians. The Cape could retain its nonracial franchise, although economic and educational restrictions precluded most from qualifying. Even with these stringent requirements, several thousand Cape coloreds and Africans could vote, but they too were not allowed to be elected to Parliament. Parliament would be for whites only. In fact, of the 152 articles of the Act of Union that were hammered out over four months of debate at the 1908–1909 National Convention, only two clauses refer to the "non-Europeans." The deplorable racial situation today in South Africa is often assumed to be completely the responsibility of the Boers, but the facts do not support such a conclusion. Although the English are often given credit for a vision of human dignity that transcended the color bar, the British practice in South Africa was much more ambiguous. Consider a 1908 memorandum from Alfred Milner's successor, William Palmer Selbourne, to Louis Botha: "The black man is absolutely incapable of rivalling the white man. . . . No one can have any experience of the two races without feeling the intrinsic superiority of the white man."[5]

The National Convention had three sessions in major centers: Durban, Cape Town, and Bloemfontein. Attended by thirty delegates—twelve from the Cape, eight from the Transvaal, five from Natal, and five from the Orange Free State (called the Orange River Colony at that time)—the convention saw its major role as preparing the way for the two dominant white groups to live together in harmony. Toward this end, key agenda items included the choice of the capital city and the selection of the official language. After considerable debate, it was clear that unanimity on the capital was impossible so the convention decided that Pretoria would be the seat of the government and Cape Town the seat of the parliament; Bloemfontein was to be the judicial capital. While the British assumed English would be the official language, the Afrikaner leaders made an eloquent plea for Dutch. The result was the adoption of the bilingual principle: "Both the English and the Dutch shall be official languages and shall be treated on a footing of equality. All records of parliament, all Bills, Acts and Notices of general public importance shall be in both languages." Only by an Act of Parliament in 1925 did the Dutch yield to Afrikaans, a hybrid of Dutch and other languages.

The 1908 National Convention set in motion the healing process for the two major white tribes, and in many ways it is a model for the unfinished business of the nation—healing the rift between black and white. When the Act of Union was heard in London for the required royal assent, Herbert Asquith, the Earl of Oxford and Asquith, made an appeal that has yet to be acted on: "South Africa, in the exercise of their undoubted and unfettered freedom, shall find it possible, sooner or later, and sooner rather than later, to modify the provisions regarding the natives."[6]

A good example revealing some of the basis of the racism of South Africa is the 1911 Mines and Works Act. Behind the black-white relationships is a concern about power. By the turn of the century, blacks were acquiring the skills to be hired in some of the better-paying jobs in the mines. Owners were interested in hiring blacks rather than bringing in whites from overseas at premium wages. However, the white laborers in mining marshaled their political and trade union power to establish a job color bar. According to the Mines and Works Act of 1911, Africans could not be employed as skilled workers in the mines. (The act was later elaborated on in 1926.)

In 1912, in response to the loss of the Cape franchise in the new Union constitution, blacks formed the South African National Native Congress, which was renamed the African National Congress (ANC) in 1917. This movement spread throughout the nation and served as the vehicle to express black discontent as well as aspirations. Its efforts were all channeled within the framework of the constitution, championing such causes as the abolition of the pass laws, urban freehold, and political, economic, and civil rights. Only much later, in the face of little response from the government, did the ANC abandon its policy of exclusively nonviolent strategies.

In 1913, in order to ensure a supply of cheap labor, Africans were barred from residing outside their "reserves." Men could work for cheap wages outside their areas while working for Europeans, for their families could survive on an agricultural economy in the reserves. By this act and a further amplification in the 1936 Natives' Trust and Lands Act, about 14 percent of the land was designated for blacks (the so-called homelands) while 86 percent was reserved for whites.

Under the tenure of Prime Minister Botha and his successor, Jan Christian Smuts, policies were designed to forge alliances with the English-speaking communities. Many, if not most, Boers did not support these moves to cooperate with the British. There was a strong current to develop an Afrikaner culture and to oppose all things British. In fact, James Barry Hertzog, the man who finally succeeded Smuts in 1924, was fired from Botha's cabinet in 1912 for so strongly opposing reconciliation with the English-speakers. In 1913, under the leadership of Hertzog, a new political party, the Nationalist Party, was formed with the popular slogan of "South Africa First." The majority of the Boers could not easily forget the atrocities of the British during the Anglo-Boer War and their goal was to gain political control of South Africa. Although in principle the new Constitution guaranteed equality between the British and the Boer, the fact was that the British had been ruling for so long that they were firmly entrenched in the top posts of the civil service, the railways, and many local governments. Afrikaans and Afrikaner culture became the vehicle to express a rising tide of Afrikaner nationalism.

Afrikaner Nationalism

The Nationalist Party, under Hertzog, finally won control of the government in 1924, and an era of Afrikaner dominance began to take shape. Whites were protected from African competition through new legislation, and a number of measures were taken to help alleviate Afrikaner poverty. Export quotas, import duties, and minimum price controls were enacted to help white farmers. In 1925, Afrikaans replaced Dutch as the official language, and with this move bilingual competencies were enforced for all civil service employees. This overturn gave Afrikaners a decided advantage, for many of the English-speakers had never bothered to learn the language of the Boers, which they disdained. Gradually Afrikaners moved from farms in the rural area to the cities, at first taking a subservient role to the English and gaining a foothold in the civil service and other quasi-government organizations. Before long they became full-fledged colleagues in business and industry.

Hertzog enacted what was called the "civilized labor" policy. The government would hire "civilized"—that is, white workers— in preference to so-called uncivilized—that is, black workers. The effect of this policy was dramatic. For example, among railway workers, in the first ten years of the Hertzog administration, the percentage of blacks dropped from 75 to 49 percent while the white percentage rose from 9.5 to 39 percent. In 1936 Hertzog passed the Representation of Natives Act, which took the 11,000 black Africans in the Cape off the common voters' roll. He also strengthened the pass laws and authorized the government to exercise "forced removals" of blacks when necessary for the convenience of white areas.

Hertzog's administration encouraged a strong current of Afrikaner nationalism. Hertzog did not advocate melding the two white cultures but rather had a vision of "twin streams" of English- and Afrikaans-speaking South Africans who could live together in harmony. In 1933 Daniel Malan broke away from Hertzog's approach to form the "Purified" Nationalist Party, which would champion the cause of an Afrikaner Republic. Malan was a member of the famous Afrikaner Broederbond, an organization founded in 1918 to safeguard Afrikaner interests. Initially, its role was to promote the culture and language and strengthen the Afrikaner identity in the face of an overwhelming British presence in the urban and business life. In a short time, however, the Broederbond became a secret organization, its chief aim being Afrikaner domination rather than preservation. Still active and most influential today, the Broederbond now has 800 branches and 12,000 members. The Afrikaner exclusiveness of Malan's new "Purified" Nationalist Party seemed to be a carbon copy of the Broederbond's agenda.[7] Malan would soon have the opportunity to implement that agenda, because he won the election for prime minister in 1948.

In order to understand the root convictions of the Nationalist Party, consider the party's rationale as detailed in a 1948 statement:

On the one hand, there is a policy of equality which advocates equal rights within the same political structure of all civilized and educated persons, irrespective of race or colour, and the gradual granting of the franchise to non-Europeans as they become qualified to make use of democratic rights. On the other hand there is the policy of separation, which has grown up from the experience of the established European population of the country, and which is based on the Christian principles of justice and reasonableness. . . . We can only act in one of two directions. Either we must follow the course of equality, which must eventually mean national suicide for the white race, or we must take the course of separation ("apartheid"), through which the character and the future of every race will be protected and safeguarded, with full opportunities for development and self-maintenance in their own ideas, without the interests of one clashing with the interests of the other.[8]

Malan, departing from the policy of all previous administrations, chose a cabinet composed completely of Afrikaners. To be sure, Malan's policies during his six-year tenure did not introduce segregation to South Africa, but they did begin a process, carried to term in successive Nationalist Party-controlled governments, that transformed a segregated way of life into a rigid ideology enforced by legal and theological sanctions.

The Legal Sanctions

From 1948 until the 1960s, the legislature passed major laws that formed what is now known as *apartheid*. Some highlights of this legislation are briefly reviewed as follows:

1949: Prohibition of Mixed Marriages Act. This law forbids interracial marriages. In 1950 an amendment to the Immorality Act forbade "irregular carnal intercourse"; that is, sexual acts between whites and blacks. (Both of these laws were repealed in 1985.)

1950: Population Registration Act. All South Africans are to be classified according to racial categories. The major categories are African, Cape Colored, Asian, and White; and some subdivisions exist. Should doubt exist as to the appropriate category for a person, the act specifies that appearance and general community acceptance be considered.

1950: Group Areas Act (amended in 1966). The keystone of separate development, this legislation zones land by race. Property and business rights are the exclusive domain of people of the specific racial group designated for the area. Once an area is designated for a particular race, all people of other races must move out. Over 100,000 families have been removed from their homes since this act was passed. In the case of Indians, often no houses were vacant, so the families stayed in a white area and consequently were prosecuted.

The Black Land Act of 1913 and the Development Trust and Land Act of 1936 provided for some 14 percent of the land for the ten "homelands" for Africans. Under the terms of the Black Administration Act of 1927, over two million Africans have been removed from white-designated areas and sent to a "homeland"; the number of blacks in white-designated areas (86 percent of the land of the country) is not to exceed the labor needs of the area.

In 1985, the government announced that no "forced removals" would be carried out while the policy is under review.

1952: Aboliton of Passes and Coordination of Documents Act. The objective of the South African government has always been to limit the number of blacks in the "white-designated" areas to that number required to run the white economy. This policy is generally referred to as the "influx control policy." The 1952 law coordinated existing pass laws and required that all Africans age sixteen years or over must carry a reference (pass) book at all times. The pass book indicates whether the holder has permission to be in a white-designated area. The founding legislation for influx control is Section 10 of the 1945 Urban Areas Consolidation Act. According to that bill, an African may not remain in a white-designated area for more than seventy-two hours unless the person has resided in that area since birth. So, for example, an African living in Soweto (a white-designated area, because it is not a homeland) can live there legally if he or she has resided there since birth. In addition, an African may legally be there if the person has worked in the area for at least ten years; if the person is the spouse of someone who is legally there, or is an unmarried daughter, or is a son if under eighteen years old.

This legislation also allows for migrant workers living in Soweto, for example, if they have a contract for some specific work with a specific employer. Contracts must be renewed yearly, and migrants must live in single-sex hostels.

They cannot bring their families with them from the homelands but are expected to visit their families monthly or whenever possible. At present, about half of the 22 million Africans live in black townships (adjoining white-designated areas), and only half of these have permanent-residence rights in those townships. Thus only a fourth of the Africans currently have free access to the labor market. In April 1986, P.W. Botha announced the abolition of the pass laws; the import of new legislation is not yet clear.

1953: *Bantu Education Act.* The act was intended to ensure that the educational system reflects the government policy of separate development. It also envisioned that Africans would have a subordinate role in the wider society, so that although Afrikaans and English would be taught in African schools, proficiency requirements would only be such that people could engage in simple conversations with Europeans about work or related matters. The tribal mother tongue was to be the medium of instruction for the first eight years. Since the education provided by the missionaries often encouraged Africans to compete directly with whites for jobs, the central government nationalized all these schools that received state funding and adjusted the curriculum to conform to the apartheid vision. Many schools run by missionaries were not able to operate without government funding and had to close after the passing of the 1953 bill. The critical shortage today of competent black teachers, managers, and community leaders is in many ways due to this bill.

In order to gain some perspective on the extent to which the government is willing to go to enforce apartheid, it may be helpful to summarize how that doctrine influences the present educational system. The magnitude and expense of the bureaucracy is outrageous. To educate children in South Africa there are ten education departments in the ten African homelands, four educational departments for white children in the four provinces, a cabinet-level minister for the education of African children in the white-designated areas, a cabinet-level minister for general educational policy, a minister of education attached to the colored chamber of Parliament and a minister of education attached to the Indian chamber of Parliament. If the cost in human suffering of this ideology were not so high, its ridiculous bureaucracy might be humorous. So far, the government's position is that educational apartheid, no matter how inefficient, inhuman, or expensive, is not negotiable.

At the present time almost all children are educated in segregated schools, which are located in segregated areas. A few church and other private schools conduct integrated classes, although even in these schools only a small number of blacks are admitted. Latest available figures show that in the 1983-1984 financial year the government spent an average of R1,654 (including capital expenditure) on white pupils, while R569 and R234 was spent on colored and black pupils respectively. Ken Hartshorne, a leading education scholar, estimates there is a seven to one disparity in the unit cost of white and black education. (One dollar was worth a little over two rands in 1986.)

1953: Reservation of Separate Amenities Act. This law—along with a number of others, including the Liquor Act of 1928, the Railways and Harbors Acts Amendment Act of 1947, the Motor Carrier Transportation Act of 1930, the State-aided Institutions Amendment Act of 1957, and the Group Areas Act—provides for wide-ranging social segregation. In recent years, the enforcement of segregations has slightly relaxed. For example, in theaters, parks, and a small number of hotels—designated ''international hotels''—blacks and whites are not segregated. Certain sports facilities and clubs are desegregated. However, many areas of life—including cinemas, buses, trains, taxis, libraries, schools, beaches, and resorts—are still segregated.

1956: Labor Relations Act. This law reaffirmed the principle that certain skilled jobs would be reserved for whites. The 1937 Industrial Conciliation Act declared that blacks could not join registered trade unions. The Mines and Works Act of 1911 had made it illegal for blacks to obtain "blasting certificates," and thus the act precluded black Africans from qualifying for a whole range of good mining jobs that require such certificates. Today blacks are still not able to obtain blasting certificates; however, this is the only racial job reservation that remains a matter of law. To be sure, much racial prejudice still exists on the part of individuals, but the Statute Book is almost clear of the color bar. In 1979, following the recommendations of the Wiehahn Commission, black workers were given the right to form or join unions. To date, this right is the major gain of Africans in the struggle for freedom.

1959: Extension of University Education Act. This act forbade the white universities to admit black students unless the course of study sought by the student was not available at a black university. Separate universities were organized in the homelands for black students on an ethnic basis. Today, the major white English universities all have some black African, colored, or Indian students, although not more than 15 percent of the enrollment in any case.

1959: Promotion of Bantu Self-Government Act. This bill provided that the small part of the country that had been set aside as native areas or Bantu homelands be divided into eight (now ten) "self-governing" national units or Bantustans. All blacks, on the basis of tribal heritage, would be assigned to one of these homelands, and voting rights would be exercised there rather than in the national Parliament. The representation of blacks in Parliament that was then operative was abolished by the terms of this law. Although it was understood that about 50 percent of Africans would continue to live in the black townships of white-designated areas, the homelands concept assured the white minority that blacks would not have any legitimate claim to voting in white South Africa. The vision of the future of then Prime Minister Hendrik Verwoerd was that the Bantu "states" would ultimately join together with white South Africa in a white-ruled South African commonwealth. Most blacks resented such a plan being imposed on them in 1959, and they continue to resent it to this day. However, they are powerless to effect substantial change at present.

In 1983, according to the Republic of South Africa Constitution Act, coloreds and Indians were given the parlimentary franchise when Parliament expanded from one to three chambers. A distinction is made between "own affairs" and "general affairs," with "general affairs" (foreign affairs, defense, security) being controlled by a cabinet composed of selected members of all three chambers, and "own affairs" being governed by the particular racial chamber. Although the white Nationalist Party maintains control under the new constitution, the party does, at least, acknowledge the citizenship of Indians and coloreds. To be sure, Indians and coloreds, for the most part, have not warmly received the new constitution; the remaining 73 percent of the population, the black Africans, have yet to receive any sort of parliamentary franchise, and coloreds and Indians are understandably reluctant to accept the franchise until all can participate. A further question exists, of whether the new constitution provides the best government for the country.

The last twenty years have been both exhilarating and frightening for South Africans. Prime Minister Verwoerd (1954–1966) led the nation in an era of unparalleled prosperity and power for South Africa. In 1960, the electorate (all white) approved by a slim majority the motion that South Africa become a republic. A short time later the nation withdrew from the British Commonwealth. For the Afrikaners, a dream had been realized—they were finally free of the British. For the English speaking, there was a sense of alienation from the world.

Opposition to the racist policies of the government continued to grow. Nelson Mandela, a law school graduate of the prestigious University of Witwatersrand, accepted a leadership role in the African National Congress. After being frustrated in all attempts to effect change through nonviolent pressure, Mandela took leadership of a group (Umkonto We Sizwe, "Spear of the Nation") that planned to use sabotage in places that would not involve danger to lives. For this and other activities, he was sentenced to life imprisonment in 1964 and remains in jail today. To counteract the growing unrest in the society, the government passed a number of laws that curtailed civil liberties. At the same time, Afrikaner entrepreneurs were emerging as a force in business life in South Africa. Until the 1960s, a tacit understanding existed that the English-speaking South Africans would run the business world while the Afrikaners would manage the government. All this changed in the mid-1960s and today the Afrikaans Institute of Commerce, the *Afrikaanse Handels-instituut*, is a powerful voice in the commercial world. Achieving success and power in business seems to have largely healed the rift between the English- and Afrikaans-speakers. Many areas of co-operation exist between the two white "tribes." With this healing, however, has arisen a renewed fear of the black threat to the nation and increasing defensiveness toward criticism of apartheid from the international community.

The nation was stunned in 1966 when Prime Minister Verwoerd was stabbed to death by a messenger in the House of Parliament. The Minister of Justice, B. J. Vorster, was elected prime minister by the National Party Caucus and continued the Nationalist Party policies. Political unrest continued. The black communities were especially angry over Pretoria's policy of sending urban black dependents to the homelands. This "endorsing out" strategy broke up families and inflamed anger. In June 1976, Soweto students rebelled, ostensibly over the mandatory use of Afrikaans in schools, but also in general condemnation of the whole system. More than 176 people were killed. Not since the 1960 Sharpeville demonstrations, where the police killed sixty-nine black Africans, had the violence been so great. Reports of police brutality were widespread, and at least one black leader who died in prison—Steve Biko—was judged (by an independent commission) to have been the victim of government negligence.

In 1978 P. W. Botha assumed the role of prime minister when Vorster retired for reasons of health. Compared to previous leaders, Botha was a reform (*verligte*, or "enlightened") Nationalist. He told his white constituency that they must "adapt or die." He dramatically increased the education budget for black Africans, dismantled more color bar legislation in the workplace, granted blacks the right to form and join unions, abolished the Mixed Marriages Act and the Immorality Act, and provided a token franchise for Indians and coloreds. However, his critics in the Progressive Federal Party (the white opposition) continue to point out that all his reform measures assume the legitimacy of ''Grand Apartheid''; that is, of a society based on ethnic groupings enforced by law. Is P. W. Botha really willing to move toward genuine power sharing with black Africans? Is he willing to form a new constitution through negotiations with all ethnic groups? These questions set the context for Chapter 3, which focuses on the various policies advocated to hasten the dismantling of Grand Apartheid.

Religious Sanctions for Separate Development

Among the 1.5 million white members of the Dutch Reformed Church today are the power brokers of government policy in the Republic. Almost all the top government officials, National Party Parliament members, provincial council members, police, and military officials as well as town council members worship in a DRC church. Although most mainstream Protestant churches and the Roman Catholic Church openly criticize the policy of separate development, the DRC does not. A brief outline of the DRC position is helpful, for it is only a slight exaggeration to say that the future of South Africa largely lies in the hands of this church.[9]

An important distinction in analyzing the teachings of a church lies in the difference between official teaching and what in fact is taught and believed by the people in the pews. In the past the DRC has functioned as a civil religion par excellence, providing the people with a religious sanction for a bold Afrikaner nationalism. The Afrikaners understood themselves as struggling for dignity and identity in the face of oppression from both the British and the African, and they found a vision, a rationale, and a source of strength in the Dutch Reformed Church. However, for this study the interesting questions are ''What is the official teaching of the DRC today on separate development? Can this official teaching still provide a religious sanction for current Nationalist Party government policies on matters governing the races?''

In 1974 the General Synod of the Dutch Reformed Church promulgated a document detailing the church's position on racial matters. Titled *Human Relations and the South African Scene in the*

Light of Scripture, the document builds its case from Scripture, focusing on the creation narratives and the protohistory of Genesis 1–11.[10] The twin themes of the unity and equality of all peoples and the ethnic diversity among peoples are taken both (1) to emerge from Scripture *and* thus (2) to be in accord with the intentions of the Creator. Consider, for example, a text from the Acts of the Apostles:

From one single stock he not only created the whole human race so that they could occupy the entire earth, but he decreed how long each nation should flourish and what the boundaries of its territory should be. And he did this so that all nations might seek the deity and, by feeling their way towards him, succeed in finding him (Acts 17:27).

Although the unity of all peoples is the ultimate destiny of ethnic groups, human sin has made diversity a fact of life that finally can be overcome only in the next world, in God's Kingdom. The story of the tower of Babel tells of the results of sin.

Now Yahweh came down to see the town and the tower that the sons of man had built. "So they are all a single people with a single language!" said Yahweh. "This is but the start of their undertakings! There will be nothing too hard for them to do. Come, let us go down and confuse their language on the spot so that they can no longer understand one another." Yahweh scattered them then over the whole face of the earth, and they stopped building the town. It was named Babel therefore, because there Yahweh confused the language of the whole earth. It was from there that Yahweh scattered them over the whole face of the earth (Gen. 11:5–9).

To be sure, the 1974 document of the Synod acknowledges that the message of the Gospel has social significance. For the DRC, rather than blurring "all distinctions among peoples" the Scriptures say Christians must ensure that diversity does not degenerate into estrangement. The document, however, in what seems to be a fatal flaw, equates "diversity" with "separation." Thus, for example, the document states, "In specific circumstances and under specific conditions the New Testament makes provision for the regulation on the basis of separate development of the co-existence of various peoples in one country."[11] Although the Christian task of avoiding estrangement in the midst of *diversity* is a manageable one, it is quite another story to overcome estrangement in the face of a rigid government policy of *separation*. The facts are that the policy of separation has brutally increased injustice and systematically destroyed the family in black African communities.

The DRC document, while clearly rejecting racism and discrimination on the basis of skin color, advocates the policy of separate development. Since apartheid is often associated with racial discrimination, the term *apartheid* is avoided. As indicated, the document expresses concern that the policy of separate development be implemented in accordance with the biblical norms of justice and love. In the face of ample evidence that this task is impossible, the DRC nevertheless refuses to abandon the policy. Why? Could it be that not biblical principles, but the survival of Afrikaner power and identity, is controlling the DRC theology? As this chapter has indicated, the policy of separate development has required a plethora of legislation demeaning to the human dignity of blacks. In fact, the one clear advantage of the legislation is that it maintains the power and privileges of the whites. To be sure, some of the most incisive criticism of the Dutch Reformed Church in South Africa has come from its own theologians. A conviction is growing in the DRC that Dutch Reformed practice is ''more determined by the interests of the Afrikaner than the Word of God.''[12]

To understand how such a fundamentally religious people as the Afrikaners could bend the Word of God to their own interests, it is well to remember that civil religion is an ever-present temptation, a temptation to which we in the United States have often succumbed.[13] The Afrikaners, in the face of great adversity, triumphed over enemeies in the major events of their history—the Great Trek, the many wars, the 1948 National Party Victory, and the 1961 founding of the republic. Through these events, many come to believe that God was acting in their history as he had done in Israel. They are a chosen people destined by God to bring an abundant life to all southern Africa. God is believed to be on their side, guiding their policies and their destiny. With this sense of divine calling and mission, central policies such as separate development are not simply strategies devised on the basis of prudential judgments. Rather, they are thought to be part of the very order of creation and hence not easily altered. As mentioned earlier, however, this overarching world view is losing its compelling power for the DRC as it becomes more and more apparent that separate development is impossible to reconcile with a biblical vision of justice and love.

One of the most hopeful signs that the process of dismantling apartheid is indeed underway is a statement released from the August 1985 annual meeting of the Presbytery of Stellenbosch of the DRC. It is worth quoting:

We recognise that, in the South African society, racial discrimination plays a fundamental role in both structural and personal matters; we confess that this is contrary to the biblical principles of love of one's neighbour and justice.

We also acknowledge that the ideal of apartheid did not succeed in creating social justice but has, on the contrary, led to human misery, frustration and injustice.

We confess that the Nederduitse Gereformeerde Kerk has often insensitively and uncritically tolerated the negative realities and consequences of apartheid.

We therefore hereby declare ourselves prepared

a) to assess the apartheid system in all its consequences truly honestly and critically:

b) with all other people in our country, to seek prayerfully for a meaningful alternative for our land, and to do whatever we can to alleviate the suffering caused by the system.[14]

To this, all Christians and people of goodwill throughout the world can only say, "Amen." Chapter 3 will outline some alternative policies advocated to reform the present state of affairs.

NOTES

1. There are a number of historical studies on South Africa, for example, see Monica Wilson and Leonard Thompson, eds., *The Oxford History of South Africa*, Vols. 1 & 2 (London: Oxford University Press, 1967 and 1971); T. R. Davenport, *South Africa: A Modern History* (London: Macmillan, 1977); C. W. de Kiewiet, *A History of South Africa: Social and Economic* (London: Oxford University Press, 1941); and Robert Lacour-Gayet, *A History of South Africa* (London: Cassell, 1977).

2. John W. de Gruchy, *The Church Struggle in South Africa* (Grand Rapids, Mich.: Eerdmans, 1979), p. 13.

3. *Ibid*. p. 19. Quoted by I. D. MacCrone, *Race Attitudes in South Africa* (London: Oxford University Press, 1937), p. 126.

4. Cf. Peter Hinchliff, *The Church in South Africa* (London: SPCK, 1968), pp. 46–47.

5. Quoted by Robert Lacour-Gayet, *A History of South Africa* (London: Cassell, 1977), p. 241.
6. *Ibid*, p. 242
7. Cf. J. Hennie Serfontein, *Brotherhood of Power* (London: Rex Collings, 1979), and Ivor Wilkins and Hans Strydom, *The Super Afrikaners* (Johannesburg: Jonathan Ball, 1978).
8. Quoted by Gideon S. Ware, *A History of South Africa* (New York: Holmes & Meier, 1974), pp. 167–8.
9. Cf. de Gruchy.
10. *Human Relations and the South African Scene in the Light of Scripture* (Cape Town: Dutch Reformed Church Publishers, 1975).
11. *Ibid.*, pp. 32f.
12. de Gruchy, p. 81. For an analysis of the development of the prophetic dimension of the church in South Africa, see Peter Walshe, *Church Versus State in South Africa* (New York: Orbis Books, 1983). See also Marjorie Hope and James Young, *The South African Churches in a Revolutionary Situation* (New York: Orbis Books, 1981).
13. For example, see Robert N. Bellah, *The Broken Covenant: American Civil Religion in Time of Trial* (New York: Seabury Press, 1975).
14. Quoted and discussed in David J. Bosch, "Reconciliation: An Afrikaner Speaks," *Leadership* 4(4), 1985, pp. 64–65 (Cape Town, South Africa).

Chapter 3

AGENDAS TO OVERCOME
APARTHEID: AN OVERVIEW

Experience teaches us that, generally speaking, the most perilous moment
for a bad government is one when it seeks to mend its ways. Only
consummate statecraft can enable a king to save his throne when, after a
long spell of oppressive rule, he sets out to improve the lot of his subjects.
Patiently endured so long as it seemed beyond redress, a grievance comes
to appear intolerable once the possibility of removing it crosses men's
minds.

Alexis de Tocqueville

After seeing apartheid through the eyes of Moses Mpunthe
and Simon Middleton in Chapter 1, and tracing the development of
the whole way of life buttressed by statutory racial discrimination
and a theological rationale in Chapter 2, the reader is now ready to
consider the various agendas proposed in South Africa to overcome
apartheid. This step is crucial, for in order to judge the ethics of
U.S. investments in South Africa and the appropriateness of certain
pressure strategies such as divestment, it is first necessary to clarify
the political agendas of the key actors in the troubled nation. In
this chapter I first outline the present South African government
position, as advanced by State President Pieter W. Botha and his
administration. Then some of the major movements in the republic
are reviewed: Gatsha Buthelezi's Inkatha, the African National Congress, the United Democratic Front, the Progressive Federal Party
(the official white opposition party), and the South African business
community. Then I discuss the various responses in the United
States to the apartheid dilemma: the U.S. government response, the
Sullivan Principles, the Free South Africa Movement, and the
churches. The stance of the United Nations is also outlined. Then
the stage will be set for Chapter 4 and its focus on a Christian
response to U.S. investments in South Africa.

Pieter W. Botha: "Cooperative Coexistence"

Analysts, both domestic and international, have long argued that P. W. Botha is increasingly alienating his potentially large, moderate constituency by the absence of any clear overall vision of the sort of society he is trying to fashion with his reform. Some whites, growing insecure at the thought of being overrun by blacks in the country, are moving to the right on the political spectrum and are resisting all change. Some moderate blacks, on the other hand, increasingly frustrated with the pace of political reform, are moving to the left and often resorting to violence in hopes of hastening their freedom. In recent years Botha has often been trapped between volleys of such reactive responses, first from the right, then from the left. The leaders in the black townships are generally thought by their constituencies to be impotent, for the people know well that the riots in Sharpeville (1960) and Soweto (1976) achieved more for the cause of reform than did any of their elected officials' activities.

Botha has been advised by many, especially the South African business community, to be less of a party politician and more of a statesman, to lead his people with a clear vision of a dynamic society that enshrines a justice that knows no color bar. At one point, Botha seemed to understand and accept the advice; officials of his administration conveyed to the U.S. government as well as to South Africa business leaders that he would advance his agenda for substantive reform at a National Party Congress in Durban on 15 August 1985. As it turned out, the Durban speech was a diatribe against other nations interfering with South African internal matters. The address not only did not restore the confidence of the moderates in his own country, but so frightened the international banking community that a financial crisis followed in short order (see Chapter 1). On 30 September 1985, however, in a speech at a party congress at Port Elizabeth, Botha delivered an address that is the closest he has come to offering his administration's vision of the future of the society.[1]

Botha candidly admits that "constitutional rights for blacks in the central government have . . . been a point of dispute in South

Africa right from the start.'' He wants to stress that the problem began long before 1948 when the National Party assumed power. Departing from Nationalist Party doctrine, Botha rejects apartheid as a solution and instead offers a new vision that he calls ''cooperative coexistence.'' His rejection of apartheid is worth quoting:

I have already repeatedly stated that if ''Apartheid'' means—
   —Political domination of one group over another,
   —The exclusion of any community from the political decision-making process
   —Injustice and inequality in the opportunities available to any community,
   —Racial discrimination and encroachment upon human dignity,
Then the South African Government shares in the rejection of the concept.[2]

Rejecting a universal franchise in a unitary state, for ''Africa taught us that it means the dictatorship of the strongest black group,'' Botha offers a vision of a federation of ''units . . . recognized on a geographic and group basis.'' While acknowledging that much is yet to be negotiated, Botha offers the following broad contours of constitutional reform:

—The Republic of South Africa forms one State. It is an explicit implication of the Government's view that independence will not be forced on the self-governing areas and that they form part of the Republic until they should decide to become independent. In this regard however, the Government also respects the decision of the four states that previously formed part of the Republic, to take independence. As a result of the large degree of interdependence between the independent states and the Republic, the Government nevertheless acknowledged the possibility of co-operation with these states in an overall framework.
—It follows this point of view that there should be one collective South African Citizenship for all who form part of the Republic. For this reason I announced on 11 September this year among other things that the South African Citizenship of those black persons who permanently reside in the Republic, but who lost their Citizenship as a result of independence, will be restored.
—Thirdly, my Government stated clearly that all groups and communities within the geographical area of this state must obtain representation to the highest level without domination of the one over the other. Therefore I do not understand why the Government is time and again still expected to say that it is prepared to share its power of decision-making with

other communities. It is accepted National Party policy and surely it is evident in views repeatedly expressed by the Government.[3]

In the Port Elizabeth speech, later amplified at Cape Town, Botha called on the President's Council, an appointed group from the three-chamber central government, to broaden its role so that blacks could be represented on a national level. Presently the President's Council is composed of sixty members; thirty-five appointed by political parties and twenty-five appointed by the president. Channels for important negotiations with black leaders are at least being discussed. In a January 31, 1986, speech to Parliament at Cape Town, Botha again spoke of this "National Statutory Council," but he failed to provide specifics of the plan and it was not well received by black leaders. In April 1986, Botha surprised many by announcing that the hated pass laws would no longer be enforced and would be abolished. Should this change actually mean that blacks can live and work where they choose, it is a major step in dismantling apartheid.

To be sure, Botha's vision is far from that of the most progressive leaders of South Africa. Continued segregation of schools, housing, and "culture" is assured. Yet the results of the off-year elections in October 1985, of the five seats up for reelection, clearly announced that Botha's political foes who oppose any changes in apartheid were gaining ground. The National Party lost only one of its seats, but its majority was reduced in three of the whites-only constituencies. Most commentators suggested that the off-year pattern tells little about the general election pattern, but they were fearful that Botha might slow the pace of reform even more. One seat was lost to the extreme right-wing Reconstituted National party; and the Conservative Party, under the leadership of Botha's old political foe, Andries P. Treurnicht, gained some ground, although no seats. Still, of the 178 seats in the white chamber, the Nationalists hold a comfortable majority with 123 members. The closest rival is the Progressive Federal Party, with 27 seats, while the Conservative Party holds a mere 18.

The Progressive Federal Party

One of the most surprising features of South African political life is the vitality and strength of the opposition party, the Progressive Federal Party. Led by a talented and articulate Afrikaner, Frederik van Zyl Slabbert, the party has championed the cause of the blacks and argued for immediate negotiations for reform. Slabbert's strong criticism of the government is regularly reported in the press in South Africa. His trenchant analysis goes to the heart of the current unrest:

Nothing is a greater threat to the rights and protection of minorities than to entrench racial and ethnic groups in a new constitutional dispensation.

This is one of the fundamental shortcomings of the Government's constitutional reforms, both in the tricameral parliament and in the latest constitutional initiatives between Black and White.

If racial and ethnic groups, as defined in law by the Government should form the building blocks of a new constitutional dispensation for South Africa, then a future picture of seige and conflict will become a reality.[4]

After hearing State President P. W. Botha's agenda for overcoming apartheid at the official opening of Parliament on January 31, 1986, Slabbert decided to resign from Parliament. "I have decided the time has come for me to go," he announced to Parliament. The Reform proposals are "not good enough—it is a false start."

As I indicated in Chapter 2, the doctrine of separate development that undergirds the new constitution is firmly rooted in the teachings of the Dutch Reformed Church, or DRC (in Afrikaans, the Nederduitse Gereformeerde Kerk, or NGK). The racial structure of the church is reflected in the sister churches of the DRC: for coloreds there is the Nederduitse Gereformeerde Sending Kerk; for black Africans, the Nederduitse Gereformeerde Kerk in Africa; and for Indians, the Reformed Church in Africa. Some DRC officials are hopeful that the 1986 General Synod will begin the moves necessary to bring structural unity to the church and end the color bias. Although only a few DRC theologians are presently arguing to open the white churches to all races, the theology of separateness is increasingly under attack. Before Slabbert's critiques find resonance in the Afrikaner way of thinking, the Dutch Reformed Church will have to mend its ways. In Slabbert's judgment, negotiations should involve "all significant interest groups," including Buthelezi, Mandela, and representatives from the ANC, United Democratic Front (UDF), Inkatha, AZAPO, and the black trade unions.

The African National Congress

For P. W. Botha, the African National Congress (ANC) is anathema. In his words, "And if communist-controlled organizations such as the ANC should have their way with support from abroad, it will be a dark day for South Africa."[5] The government's position on the ANC was outlined in a speech by the Deputy Minister of Information, D. J. Louis Nel.[6] In essence, he said, the ANC is a "terrorist and Communist backed organization" whose stated aim is "the total disruption of the Black communities."

In the government's view, the ANC is seeking total change through violence and revolution and has formed "an alliance with the South African Communist Party, who endeavor to establish a Marxist-Socialist state in South Africa." The ANC does not want a reform that would result "in the sharing of power by all South Africans irrespective of race, colour or creed," but it seeks a revolution and the "seizing of power by a militant few," according to Nel. "These organisations contrive incident after incident, muster crowds to go on the rampage and see to it that the eyes of the world via television are fixed upon them." Addressing a Youth Year rally in Bloemfontein, P. W. Botha reiterated a common theme: much of the campaign against South Africa comes from supporters around the world of the "godless Marxist ideology."[7]

For their part, ANC leaders Nelson Mandela and Oliver Tambo have always claimed that they are not communists. They have accepted money and arms from the Soviet Union and cooperation from the small South African Communist Party. Norway and Sweden contribute substantial funds for nonmilitary ANC programs, and it is reported that the ANC raises almost $30 million a year around the globe. According to its leaders, ANC violence only began in the 1960s in response to the government's violence. For the most part, the ANC uses sabotage designed to provoke the government and raise the anxiety of the white citizenry. In 1980, an attack on the Sasol oil installations was given wide publicity, and in 1984, forty-four bombing incidents were attributed to the ANC.

The Bible of the ANC is the Freedom Charter, a document that renounces apartheid and calls for a multiracial democracy. Drawn up by a "Congress of the People" in June 1955, the charter would, if implemented, pose a considerable threat to the present economic arrangements of South Africa: "The national wealth shall be restored to the people. The mineral wealth, the banks and monopoly industry, shall be transferred to the ownership of the people as a whole."[8]

Most blacks identify with Nelson Mandela and the ANC; they see this approach as the most tangible way to oppose apartheid. Surveys of the black community continue to indicate Mandela as the people's choice for leadership. Having been jailed for over twenty years, he is often thought of as a hero or martyr. The ANC has come to symbolize the struggle for freedom against oppression for most blacks. Whether most blacks subscribe to the full program of the ANC, or even understand what that program entails is quite another matter.

It seems highly unlikely that the ANC or any single group is coordinating or directing the widespread violence across South Africa. Such an accusation would be attributing far too much credit to their organizational skills; credit they would willingly accept, no doubt. On the contrary, most analysts believe that the violence in the black townships is largely caused by the frustration against the system, triggered by many situations and circumstances that heighten the tension. Because many blacks have been co-opted in recent years to administer apartheid in the townships, they have become targets of the violence. If P. W. Botha's reform program actively involved black leaders and moved at a quicker pace, I believe the level of violence would dramatically decrease.

A growing number of whites in South Africa have come to see the fallacy of the Botha government's position on the ANC. A prominent Dutch Reformed cleric, former theology professor at the University of Stellenbosch and member of the Broederbond, the Rev. Nico Smith, asked permission to lead a delegation of clerics to meet the leaders of the outlawed ANC in the exiled headquarters at Lusaka, Zambia. The government refused his request, but Smith made his point: the government should be meeting with the ANC! Eight students at Stellenbosch University, long the training ground for Afrikaner leaders, announced plans to travel to Lusaka to meet representatives of the ANC. The government responded by withdrawing the students' passports.

A month later, in November 1985, the editor of the *Cape Times* newspaper, Tony Heard, published an interview with exiled ANC president Oliver Tambo. Since Tambo is a "banned person" he may not be quoted, according to South Africa's very restrictive security laws, without the permission of the Minister of Law and Order. For publishing the interview, Heard was charged under the Internal Security Act and could receive as much as a three-year jail sentence. The interview itself was quite instructive, belying many governmental stereotypes of the ANC and showing that a genuine chance existed for political negotiations. In Tambo's words, "There is always the possibility of a truce. It would be very, very easy, if, for example, we started negotiations."[9] Even if the ANC leaders cannot be trusted, as many argue, it is difficult to understand what would be lost in attempting discussions.

The United Democratic Front

In 1983, the President's Council was proposing the outlines of a tricameral parliament (subsequently adopted and implemented in 1984). At the same time, the so-called Koornhof Bills—legislation designed to strengthen the government's control over black labor—were being discussed. Mobilized in opposition to these government moves, a number of groups came together to pool their resources and offer a united front for a free, democratic, and multiracial country. Today the United Democratic Front (UDF) is a coalition of some 600 groups—political clubs, professional societies, student organizations, community groups, and labor unions. Founded by the World Alliance of Reformed Churches president, Allan Boesak, the UDF sees its role as one of coordinating the actions of the organizations. With perhaps as many as 2 million members, the group actively seeks to abolish apartheid and install majority rule.

Since the state of emergency was declared in July 1985, many UDF leaders have been detained in jails across the nation. The government has repeatedly claimed that the UDF is a front for the banned ANC. Although the UDF *has* adopted the ANC Freedom Charter, and many former members of the ANC are now members of the UDF, it is not clear that the accusation is correct.

The underlying concern of the UDF is that the Nationalist Party government is involved in an effort to modernize apartheid, not to abolish it. In the UDF's view, the Koornhof Bills attempted to divide blacks, giving urban blacks more rights and security and pushing "homeland" blacks out of the mainstream economic and political community of South Africa. In this way, the argument goes, whites could appease the international community and yet still retain control. The new constitution, similarly, is seen as an instrument of neo-apartheid.

To the left of the UDF is the Azanian People's Organization (AZAPO), a black consciousness group opposed to any sort of multiracial government. For members of this movement, the proper name of the country known as South Africa is Azania, a Greek form of the Persian word *zanj-bar* (Zanzibar) meaning "land of the blacks." Founded in 1978 after other black organizations were banned, AZAPO is a relatively small group of blacks. In 1983 AZAPO brought 200 organizations together and formed the National Forum (NF), which declared its intention to abolish apartheid along "with the system of racial capitalism." Considerably to the left of the UDF, the NF is locked in a struggle against "the system of racial capitalism which holds the people of Azania in bondage for the benefit of the small minority of white capitalists and their allies, the white workers and the reactionary sections of the black middle class."[10] In many black townships, internecine violence flares up between members of the UDF and AZAPO, each fighting for community dominance.

Mangosuthu Gatsha Buthelezi and Inkatha

Mangosuthu Gatsha Buthelezi, popularly known as Gatsha Buthelezi, is thought by many to be the most impressive black leader in South Africa today. Although I had already read much that was positive about him and had analyzed his program of political reform, my very affirmative judgment is largely the result of conversations with him over a period of one day. He is well read, highly intelligent and politically astute. As the hereditary leader of the South Africa's 6 million Zulus, Chief Buthelezi is the chief minister of the Kwazulu homeland administration and extremely popular with the Zulus, most of whom live in or near the "homeland," which is laced throughout Natal. As indicated in Chapters 1 and 2, the original plan of the National Party was to gradually have all the so-called homelands constitutionally separate from South Africa. Buthelezi has repeatedly taken a bold stand against independence and has argued for sharing power with the white government.

Buthelezi's power base in South Africa is a highly organized black political organization known as Inkatha (the full title is Inkatha Yenkululeko Yesizwe, which means the "National Cultural Liberation Movement"). Today Inkatha is a million-member organization, predominantly Zulu but open to all blacks. Most members of Inkatha are in one of the areas of Kwazulu, although branches operate throughout the Transvaal townships, the Orange Free State, and Cape Town. As president of Inkatha, Buthelezi is in a position to hold genuine negotiations with the Nationalist government. His positions are developed in dialogue with representatives of the over one thousand branches of Inkatha and thus reflect grass-roots thinking.

Buthelezi's positions are well known throughout South Africa, having been discussed in the press and university circles. A central tenet is that the National Party must be prepared to discuss "power sharing" before Buthelezi will sit down at the negotiating table. The government has always wanted to talk about "power division," and for blacks this means a "homeland"-type situation where the whites control 87 percent of the land and the blacks control 13 percent. On the contrary, Buthelezi argues that "there is no decision taken by the South African Government which does not affect the lives of every one of the country's citizens." The new constitution is fundamentally unacceptable in that it divides interests into "own affairs" and "general affairs." "Bits and pieces of power have been divided among the so-called homelands. Bits and pieces of power have also been allocated, in principle if not yet in practice, to the black local authorities in the common area. No power has been shared."[11]

Inkatha and indeed all blacks will never renounce their ultimate ideal of South African citizenship and a franchise in the national political institutions. Buthelezi has repeatedly stated that while his ideal is one-person-one-vote, he would come to the negotiating table prepared to shelve a unitary one-person-one-vote system in order to make a negotiated future possible. From 1980 to 1982, a special commission appointed by the Kwazulu legislative assembly met to consider some steps that might move blacks toward their ideal. Called the Buthelezi Commission, the group was composed of key leaders of business, religion, and academia. Such distinguished figures as Harry Oppenheimer and Archbishop Denis Hurley served on the commission. The final report suggested an experiment in multiracial government that would bring together the white provincial administration of Natal and the black administration of Kwazulu. The next step proposed, after developing mutual trust on the administrative level, would be to form a multiracial regional legislature replacing the two segregated chambers.

Although the commission recommended elections by universal franchise, their model of democracy was a "consensus" model rather than a "majoritarian" or Westminster model. This choice was to ensure that the white minority—the white, Indian, and colored populations combined would still be only 25 percent of the total population of Natal and Kwazulu—would not be committing the "political suicide" so feared by P. W. Botha. The consensus model offers proportional representation rather than a plurality or winner-take-all election system. The commission recommended proportional representation in the regional legislature and cabinet, a veto possibility for legislation considered unacceptable to the interests of one group, and a bill of rights with an independent judiciary. The plan also called for the gradual phasing out of (1) land zoned by race (Group Areas Act) and (2) the influx control laws. The commission envisioned Natal-Kwazulu as a federal component of a South African state with all residents having a common citizenship.

The kind of power sharing delineated in this proposed Natal-Kwazulu multiracial regional government is what Buthelezi hopes will ultimately characterize all South Africa. At that time blacks will have parliamentary representation. As a starter, however, the report suggests that the regional experiment, run successfully, could persuade whites that power ought to be shared in all the national institutions as well.

The commission's report has received accolades from many quarters in South Africa, but the government has not accepted its proposals, though many feel that President Botha is moving toward accepting Buthelezi's initiative. Time will tell. To date, Botha's public statements are sufficiently ambiguous so that it is unclear whether he accepts "power sharing" as defined by Buthelezi. To many, the Botha rhetoric still has the ring of the old "power division."

Originally Buthelezi was a member of the ANC, and he still supports the principles of the movement as enunciated by its founding fathers in 1912. However, he has repeatedly expressed misgivings about the ANC strategy of violence which it adopted after 1960. He is also critical of the UDF and the AZAPO Movement because of their avowed intentions to make the country ungovernable and their failure to condemn black-on-black violence in South Africa. In a recent address, he succinctly stated his position:

In looking at Black political organisations in South Africa, one must realize that differences in tactics and strategies are related to visions of the future. The ANC's Mission in Exile aims to establish a revolutionary government presiding over a Marxist State. The United Democratic Front aims to establish a popular government over a socialist state and they share this view of the future with AZAPO, although they differ with each other about terminology, and are in fact killing each other, and differ about the role of Blacks in the struggle. All three of them are anticapitalist and all three of them share at minimum the view that the country must be made ungovernable so that we can start from scratch with social, political and economic engineering.[12]

Buthelezi has long been an advocate of the free enterprise system as the best means to improve the quality of life for blacks in South Africa. In this light, his repeated condemnation of the disinvestment lobby is understood. On the contrary, Buthelezi champions new investments and travels around the globe encouraging business to come to the nation. He recognizes that his view "is rejected vehemently by the ANC's Mission in Exile, by the UDF and by AZAPO." While not denying the validity of some of these groups' critiques, Buthelezi is more hopeful and more pragmatic than they are: "I am committed to tactics and strategies which will work today and which will not prejudice tomorrow, and I say simply that leaders in South Africa have no option but to let the day after tomorrow look after itself."[13]

In spite of Buthelezi's repeated criticism of the Botha administration's meager reform efforts and in spite of his courageous opposition to any attempts to constitutionally separate Kwazulu from South Africa, his pragmatic opposition to apartheid is sometimes misunderstood by some blacks. This is because he serves as Chief Minister of the Kwazulu homeland which is regarded by some blacks as an apartheid structure. However, it must be noted that throughout Zulu history Buthelezi's ancestors had served as Chief Minsters to Zulu kings many centuries before the birth of apartheid in South Africa. In my experience in South Africa, in the province of Natal Buthelezi is clearly the peoples' choice for their leader. In Natal, almost all blacks to whom I spoke had great respect and admiration for him.

Outside of Natal, however, Nelson Mandela seems to be far more popular with the typical black. Most black urban youths of Soweto, for example, are convinced that Nelson Mandela and his aggressive and sometimes violent stand against the government is the only approach that will finally bring power sharing. Through Mandela, they identify with the ANC. Without the great heroic figure of Mandela, it is questionable whether the ANC could hold the allegiance of such a large number of blacks as it does today. To be sure, it is perhaps not a matter of one or the other. South Africa needs far more men and women of the character and vision exemplified by both Nelson Mandela and Gatsha Buthelezi.

The Churches in South Africa and Strategies for Change

As indicated in Chapter 2, the Dutch Reformed Church has the largest white population of all the churches in South Africa. Within the DRC are three denominations, each having racially separate bodies. The three white denominations of the DRC are the NGK (Nederduitse Gereformeerde Kerk) with 1.8 million members; the NHK (Nederduitsche Hervormde Kerk), a more conservative church with 250,000 members; and the Gereformeerde Kerk, an ultraconservative denomination with 125,000 members. As discussed in Chapter 2, the DRC (in this case, both the NGK and the NHK) makes a distinction between racism and the policy of separate development, the former being sinful and the latter being quite acceptable. Since the NGK and the NHK would not condemn apartheid as a sin and a heresy, as the nonwhite branches of the NGK with some 1.8 million members had done, the World Alliance of Reformed Churches suspended them from membership. A growing minority of NGK members want to move toward a multiracial church and society. As of yet, however, no support exists in the DRC white bodies for disinvestment or any other pressure strategies.

The major Protestant denominations show a prophetic shift in the social action agenda. As mentioned earlier, however, very few of the whites in these denominations have much power and influence in the government. Besides, their numbers are relatively small as the following table shows.

	WHITES	BLACKS	COLOREDS	ASIANS
Anglicans	450,000	800,000	350,000	9,000
Methodists	400,000	1,500,000	140,000	4,000
Presbyterians	130,000	360,000	8,000	2,000
Lutherans	40,000*	700,000	100,000	1,000
Roman Catholics	400,000	1,700,000	260,000	21,000

*In 1984 the Lutheran World Federation (LWF) suspended the Evangelical Lutheran Church of Southern Africa for its failure to reject apartheid.

These and other mainline Protestant denominations present in smaller numbers in South Africa are joined together in the South African Council of Churches (SACC). The SACC has a long history of opposition to racism and apartheid. In conjunction with the Christian Institute, an ecumenical center, SACC sponsored a series of studies on apartheid. In a 1976 report, SACC proposed a code of conduct for industries operating in South Africa. Consisting of seventeen provisions, six of which are taken from the Sullivan Code, the emphasis is on affirmative action strategies to better the lot of blacks.

In 1978 Bishop Tutu was elected general secretary of SACC. He repeatedly employed a strategy of using the *threat* of disinvestment, as well as other political and economic pressures, as a way to persuade the white government to negotiate with the blacks. In the face of much opposition, he courageously condemns violence and seeks out alternative strategies to pressure for changes in the government's racist policies. In 1985 Beyers Naude assumed the general secretary post at SACC. A former minister of the Dutch Reformed Church (NGK section), Naude was "banned" for seven years (1977–1984) for his work with the Christian Institute. Banning consists of a government order that restricts a person's rights. In Naude's case, the banning order forbade him to speak in public, meet with more than two persons at once, and be quoted in the media. Naude, like Tutu, sees the threat of disinvestment as a way to avoid violence: "I believe that under certain circumstances a Christian is morally justified to ask for disinvestment in the same way as he is morally justified to call, for instance, for strike, boycott or a radical peaceful measure in order to avert a greater danger."[14] In April 1986, in hopes of increasing the pressure on the South African government to dismantle apartheid, Bishop Tutu made a dramatic plea for global economic sanctions against the Republic.

The Roman Catholic Church too has had a long history of opposing apartheid. While strong among the blacks, the Catholic Church has not had much influence on the consciences of the white policymakers in South Africa. Membership includes 21,000 Indians, 260,000 coloreds, 1.7 million blacks, and 400,000 whites. The president of the Southern Africa Catholic Bishops' Conference, Archbishop Denis E. Hurley, O.M.I., Archbishop of Durban, is an unusually talented churchman. I was his guest during a week of interviews with a number of people in Durban, and I had the good fortune to spend many hours with him. Although, out of concern for the poor, the bishops' conference has adopted a very cautious approach to economic sanctions, it has taken prophetic stands on forced removals, the police conduct in townships, and the situation in Namibia.

The government has long had an adversarial relationship with mainstream Protestant churches and the Catholic Church. In 1984, in a case widely covered in the international as well as the South African media, Archbishop Hurley was charged with making untrue and defamatory statements about Koevoet, the police counterinsurgency unit in Namibia. Officially charged under Section 27B of the Police Act of 1979, Archbishop Hurley pleaded not guilty and was fully prepared to document the injustice. After six months of harassment, the government finally withdrew the charges, saying it "had based its case on an erroneous news report." It is perhaps an understatement to say that church-state relations for the mainstream churches are tense in South Africa. An excerpt from the archbishop's statement after the withdrawal of charges summarizes the stance of these churches: "These people fail to accept that political behaviour is subject to the moral law. It is the church's duty to promote good ethical behaviour in politics as much as in personal life."[15]

Labor Unions and the Dismantling of Apartheid

Today more than 10 percent of black workers belong to African trade unions and many commentators on the South African scene believe that the recognition of these unions by the government marked the beginning of the end of apartheid. After the riots in Soweto in 1976, the government, responding to increasing pressure from the business community, formed several commissions to study public policies relating to black workers. One of the commissions was specifically charged to make recommendations regarding the reform of labor legislation concerning Africans. Led by a scholar in industrial relations from Pretoria, Nicholas Wiehahn, the commission suggested major reforms including that Africans be allowed to join registered trade unions. In 1979, this Wiehahn Commission recommendation was accepted by the government.

Unlike labor unions in the United States, African trade unions cannot resort to the political arena to achieve goals that they do not gain through collective bargaining. Without the franchise, collective bargaining for Africans is their only access to the levers of power. Thus, for example, demanding (during the collective bargaining process) housing near the working site is a way for workers without the franchise to try to change the Group Areas Act. Similarly, when public policy does not outlaw discriminatory hiring and promotion practices, these matters become part of the collective bargaining agenda. Job security is another issue that takes on crucial importance in South Africa; if a black African is dismissed, within seventy-two hours he or she must leave the urban area where he or she resides and return to a "homeland." As might be imagined, the collective bargaining process is being asked to air grievances well beyond the competence of many industrial managers. With this overburden in mind, most businesses in South Africa are aggressively lobbying the government to improve the broad spectrum of social and political rights for the workers. For many employers, the level of black discontent is alarming. Lawrence Schlemmer, a professor at the University of Natal, found that "a majority of over 6 out of 10 blue-collar production feel either unhappy or angry about life."[16] Some of the major concerns of these workers were the cost of living, political circumstances, and wages.

The Council of Unions of South Africa (CUSA) has actively supported certain kinds of divestment. Many union federations, however, are considerably more qualified, wanting to exploit the threat of divestment for all the leverage possible but not desiring to increase unemployment.

In December 1985, thirty-six labor unions with a combined membership of more than 500,000 workers formed a new labor federation, the Congress of South African Trade Unions (COSATU). COSATU's president, Elijah Barayi, made it clear that the federation had a primarily political agenda, including abolition of the pass laws, disinvestment by foreign companies, and nationalization of the mines. COSATU member unions are some of the largest in South Africa: the Federation of South Africa Trade Unions (FOS-ATU), the National Union of Mineworkers, and the General and Allied Workers Union. The formation of this federation may herald a new militancy in the struggle for political rights.

Other black labor unions take another perspective on the issue. Lucy Mvubelo, general secretary of the largest black trade union in South Africa, the National Union of Clothing workers, opposes all economic sanctions:

To proponents of isolation, disinvestment, and embargoes, I must say: Don't break off contact, and don't advocate disengagement and withdrawal of foreign investments. Only indigenous movements—the trade unions, the political groupings, the schools, the business associations—within South Africa can bring about significant, positive change. Outsiders can influence it, but only through participation, not by isolation.[17]

Clearly, we have not heard the last word from South African black trade unions. As they grow in membership and gain experience in the use of power, unions will be a major force in the struggle for black rights.

The South African Business Community

P. W. Botha made history in 1979 when he called together leaders of the business community of South Africa at the now famous Carlton Conference and offered a vision of new cooperation between the private and public sectors. In the United States, business and government officials are accustomed to working together, and high government posts are often awarded to business executives. For important historical reasons, this sort of collaboration has not been the rule in South Africa.

When the Afrikaner National Party came to power in 1948, the business leaders were largely English-speaking whites who were deeply resented by the new rulers. This resentment, stemming from years of British imperialism and the brutal Anglo-Boer war, became entrenched in habits that maintained sharp divisions between business and government, even though a number of Afrikaners have emerged as major business leaders in recent decades. In any event, a new era was heralded when President Botha outlined a partnership where government would support the free-enterprise system by creating a climate of confidence and stability and by removing statutory racial discrimination that prevented full participation of blacks in the economy. For its part, the private sector was charged to ensure economic growth that would create much-needed jobs for the expanding population.

In the face of massive unrest in the society, six years after the Carlton Conference, it is clear that the honeymoon is over for business and government. Frederick du Plessis, chairman of Sanlam, a major conglomerate in South Africa, summed up the business response to the Botha administration when he likened the country to a car without a driver. Gavin Relly, chairman of one of the larger firms, the Anglo-American Corporation, stated the challenges: "it is necessary for the government to enter into negotiations with representatives of all groups in South Africa for a system of genuine power sharing."[18] The Association of Chambers of commerce (ASSOCOM), the South African Federated Chamber of Industries (FCI), the National African Federated Chamber of Commerce (NAFOC), and the Afrikaanse Handels-Instituut (AHI) have all called upon the government to "negotiate with acknowledged black leaders about power sharing." The business leaders have also made public a number of political reforms considered essential, such as abolishing separate educational systems for racial groups, improving housing for blacks, stopping forced removals of blacks from "white-designated" areas, abolishing the pass laws, and making all blacks citizens of South Africa.

That leading citizens should champion such desperately needed reforms is not particularly unusual in a society, but that business as an institution of society should be on the leading edge of social change is remarkable and perhaps unparalleled. To demonstrate their resolve, ninety major companies in South Africa put an advertisement in the leading newspapers of the nation in September 1985 listing their agenda for reform. Robin Lee, managing director and chief executive of the Urban Foundation in South Africa (a foundation funded by business to improve the welfare of blacks) summed up the new mood of business: "what is needed now is almost a quantum leap from conventional views of corporate social responsibility . . . to a definite, organized and visible role in bringing about rapid social and economic change."[19]

As if to demonstrate how rapid and how dramatic a change the business community envisioned, on 13 September 1985 eighteen of South Africa's most prominent business and media leaders traveled to Lusaka, Zambia, to meet with the ANC. Tony Bloom, chairman of the Premier Group, expressed well the point the delegation was trying to make: "I believe the ANC are people with whom serious negotiations can be undertaken."[20] Business leaders present were Gavin Relly, Hugh Murray, Tony Bloom, Peter Sorour, Zach de Beer, Tertius Myburgh, and Harold Pakendorf. Oliver Tambo, Chris Hani, Pallo Jordan, James Stuart, Thabo Mbeki, and Mac Maharaj represented the African National Congress. While Gavin Relly was quick to point out that "immediate universal suffrage, with no protection for minorities or safeguards for institutions" (a demand of the ANC) would never be acceptable, he did acknowledge that the meeting was valuable and laid the groundwork for "constructive

understanding." Most in South Africa hope for national conciliation, and many believe that the business community has blazed the
trail that the government must follow.

Overcoming Apartheid: The U.S. Responses

For a variety of reasons, concern over apartheid has recently moved
to center stage in the United States but the issue is by no means a
new one for Americans. In 1912 the National Association for the
Advancement of Colored People (NAACP) helped what later became the African National Congress of South Africa. Americans
for South African Resistance came together in 1952; later called
the American Committee on South Africa, the organization coor-
dinates the liberation movements of South Africa with U.S. supporters. In the 1950s, U.S. blacks began to focus their movement
for freedom in the civil rights campaigns. The 1960s saw many
black dreams come to fruition in legislation enacted by the Johnson
administration—however, not without major disturbances in most
large urban areas of the nation. The 1960s also was the era when
activists—college students, civil rights leaders, and church groups—
began exerting pressure against endowments that held investments
in firms operating in South Africa and banks that made loans to the
South African government. The goal of the activists was to eventually dismantle apartheid through pressuring the RSA government.

In 1970 the Securities and Exchange Commission gave activists
a new tool for their negotiating kit when it allowed public-interest
shareholder resolutions. Since that ruling, over 250 resolutions relating to South Africa have been introduced by activists to almost
a hundred corporations.[21] Resolutions have requested a variety of
actions from companies, such as providing information on the firm's
operations in the RSA, endorsing the Sullivan Principles, withhold-
ing new investments, suspending the sale of strategic materials to
the government, ceasing all bank loans, and actually closing all
South African branches of the firm.

While most of the resolutions fail to win more than 2 or 3 percent
of the shares voted, their high visibility has clearly had an impact
in educating business and the public about the difficult moral issues
involved with operating in South Africa. The great majority of

shareholder resolutions pertaining to South Africa are presented by church groups aligned with the Interfaith Center on Corporate Responsibility (ICCR), a coordinating and resource center of the National Council of Churches. The ICCR is an ecumenical coalition of fourteen Protestant denominations and 220 Catholic dioceses and religious orders founded in 1973 to research and coordinate the shareholder activity of member churches.

Before considering the contemporary discussion in the United States about overcoming apartheid, a brief summary of U.N. activity is helpful. Although in 1945 Prime Minister Jan Smuts was one of the founders of the United Nations, since 1952 the world organization has taken a stand against South Africa; dozens of U.N. resolutions have condemned apartheid and recommended sanctions. The U.N. Security Council initiated an arms embargo against South Africa in 1963, and in 1977 the embargo was made mandatory. Since then South Africa's arms manufacturer, ARMSCOR, has grown to become the third largest company in the nation, with a production capability of such a size that the RSA is today a net arms exporter.

The African National Congress and the Pan-Africanist Congress of Azania have limited observer status in the United Nations and can speak in the Assembly; they have also received financial support. Although resolutions have been considered in the Security Council to expel South Africa from the United Nations, American, British and French vetoes have repeatedly blocked the move. Today only twenty-nine nations have diplomatic relations with this pariah nation. Recently the U.N. General Assembly renewed its request that the Security Council adopt a whole array of sanctions against South Africa under Chapter VII of the U.N. Charter. The majority of member states supported disinvestment by multinational businesses, but the Security Council nations have refused to approve mandatory international sanctions. Although the United States has voted against the sanction resolutions, it has always made it clear that ''the American people and the U.S. Government abhor apartheid.''

The Reagan Administration: The Move from Constructive to Active Engagement

For the last thirty years, U.S. policy toward South Africa has attempted to walk a fine line between, on the one hand, taking any action that would seriously affect economic ties with the nation and, on the other hand, appearing to condone the system of apartheid. Republican and Democratic administrations alike stressed the economic and strategic importance of the land, but also realized the serious moral and perhaps political problem of identifying too closely with the white racist rulers.[22]

President Carter, while not severing any significant economic ties, pushed the anti-apartheid pole to the limit with his public hostility to the regime. Ambassador Andrew Young even offered advice to the blacks from his own experience in Georgia. While the blacks in South Africa may not have made the gains in political and economic rights during the Carter administration that they had hoped for, they at least had confidence that the United States was on their side. Perhaps more important, U.S. blacks knew that their government stood squarely opposed to racism in South Africa.

During the 1980 presidential campaign, a Georgetown University professor of African history, Chester Crocker, wrote a biting critique of Jimmy Carter's policies in South Africa. Published in the journal *Foreign Affairs*, Crocker charged that the limited leverage we have for change in South Africa was economic, and that the way to affect change was not through public hostility but rather constructive engagement.[23] Crocker advocated (1) quiet diplomacy with the present government and (2) social responsibility initiatives, on the part of business, geared to advancing blacks. In the Reagan victory in 1980, Crocker was named assistant secretary of state for African affairs. The goals of the administration for the region were threefold: to encourage a peaceful process toward democracy, to curtail the expansion of Soviet influence, and to facilitate peace between South Africa and the black states of the region.

Crocker's reasoning was that if the United States could help bring peace and stability to Mozambique, Angola, and Namibia, then, free from external threats, South Africa could focus on reforming its domestic scene. Namibia was a German colony at the end of World War I and was given to South Africa under terms of the League of Nations. In 1966 the United Nations directed that Namibia be given independence. After no action, the U.N. General Assembly in 1978 passed Resolution 435, mandating free elections in Namibia supervised by the United Nations. South African troops have been in periodic armed conflict with Namibia's South-West African People's Organization (SWAPO), and by 1981 Pretoria seemed ready for a settlement. To this day, resolution 435 has not been implemented, largely because South Africa believes Namibian independence would pose a threat to the region.

To the north of Namibia in Angola camp 30,000 Cuban troops and, in the Botha administration's view, this is the major subversive influence in the region. If the troops left Angola, Namibian independence would be much less threatening for South Africa. Jonas Savimbi, leader of the National Union forces, is an opponent of the current Marxist-backed government of Angola. The United States has refused to back Savimbi overtly, in the face of U.S. right-wing advocacy of his cause, in hopes of setting the climate for the Cuban troop departure. In any event, Crocker was instrumental in forging agreements between Angola-Namibia and South Africa (the Lusaka Accord), and Mozambique and South Africa (the Nkomati Accord). Violence across the borders has diminished, and there is some chance that the frail governments of Angola and Mozambique can survive.

Critics argue that the flaw in Crocker's approach was the assumption the Afrikaners would ever dismantle apartheid without being pressured. Many said that to assume that when the "quest for security" was realized the changes in apartheid would come is to misread the Afrikaner. To show good faith, the Reagan administration softened some of Carter's sanctions. Exports were again allowed, some of which fell in the "gray area"; for example, nonlethal military hardware. Trade and investment were encouraged. U.S. companies were granted licenses to service a major nuclear power plant. Perhaps most important, the tone of U.S. rhetoric toward South Africa changed dramatically from open hostility to understanding, if not friendship. On 9 September 1985, Reagan was forced to toughen his stance, a move he characterized as "active" engagement as opposed to "constructive" engagement.[24] The events leading to this important policy shift merit attention.

Examining the level of U.S. involvement in the anti-apartheid struggle over the last thirty years reveals a close correlation with the major events of South African government repression widely reported in the media. The shooting of demonstrators in Sharpeville in 1960, the Soweto riots in 1976, and the death of African leader Steve Biko in 1977 were all catalysts that revived the dormant U.S. movement. History will perhaps remember 1984 as *the* year when the movement took on a whole new and powerful life. This was the year the press reported the acceptance of the new RSA constitution with its tricameral Parliament and the intense anger of black South Africa over being denied any franchise. These events prepared the way for renewed U.S. fervor.

On 21 November 1984, shortly after Ronald Reagan's landslide victory over presidential contender Walter Mondale, three prominent black leaders, concerned over the arrest of 16 trade union leaders in South Africa, staged a protest at the South African Embassy. The three—Civil Rights Commission member Mary Frances Berry, Washington, D.C.; Congressman Walter Fauntroy; and Trans African executive director Randall Robinson—were arrested for demonstrating within 500 feet of the embassy. They were released, but their protest, covered by television and newspapers, caught on, and since then prominent blacks and whites have turned up at the embassy to be arrested in ritual fashion. Over 3,000 people have participated including Senator Lowell Weicker (Republican, Connecticut); eighteen members of Congress; and such personalities as Harry Belafonte, Stevie Wonder, Dick Gregory, and Amy Carter. This ritual event seems to have captured the minds and hearts of Americans or, at the very least, it has tapped into the powerful moral sentiments that the anti-apartheid movement evokes for Americans.

Randall Robinson and his colleagues named the movement the Free South Africa Movement. From examining the roster of key Jewish, Catholic, black, labor union, and Democratic Party leaders who took their turns getting arrested at the embassy door, it was clear to many that the anti-apartheid issue might be just what was needed to bring the old Democratic coalition together. The South African government, sadly, continued to provide grist for the mill by well-publicized arrests and shootings in the black townships. In a move that bitterly divided the conservative movement in the United States, thirty-five House Republicans, in December 1985, bolted from the Reagan policy and published a letter to the South African ambassador, threatening sanctions unless substantial action was taken:

We are, for the most part, politically conservative and as conservatives recognize all too well the importance and strategic value of South Africa. We understand the need for stability both within the internal affairs of your country and your external relationship with the United States. But precisely because we do feel strongly about our mutual interests, we cannot condone policies of apartheid which we believe weaken your long-term interests and certainly our ability to deal with you in a constructive manner.

The Reagan Administration has dealt with your nation on the basis of "constructive engagement." That policy merits our support as long as real steps toward complete equality for all South Africans are ongoing. If "constructive engagement" becomes in your view an excuse for maintaining the unacceptable status quo, it will quickly become an approach that can engender no meaningful support among American policymakers.

We are looking for an immediate end to the violence in South Africa accompanied by a demonstrated sense of urgency about ending apartheid. If such actions are not forthcoming, we are prepared to recommend that the U.S. government take the following two steps:

1. Curtail new American investment in South Africa unless certain economic and civil rights guarantees for all persons are in place.

2. Organize interantional diplomatic and ecoonomic sanctions against South Africa.[25]

Vin Weber (Republican, Minnesota), leader of the conservative group, stressed that they were responding to "a genuine moral issues," but also an issue with a political dimension. The representatives' support for sanctions was partially based on the need to make clear that they, in no way, wanted to appear to tolerate racism. The House had long been accustomed to Democrats William Gray of Pennsylvania and Stephen Solarz of New York leading the fight for sanctions, but when the likes of Republicans Jack Kemp (New York) and Newt Gingrich (Georgia) joined the cause there was a feeling that indeed the tide had turned.

By the summer of 1985, it was clear that "constructive engagement" was dead. The House passed a tough anti-apartheid sanctions bill by a vote of 295 to 127 in June, and the following month the Senate passed their version of the bill with an 80-to-12 vote. President P. W. Botha, almost as if he were working for the anti-apartheid lobby, imposed a state of emergency on 19 July 1985, with dramatic fanfare. It was clear to all in the United States that there would soon be a sanctions bill. On September 9, President Reagan, realizing that Congress probably had the votes to counter a veto, signed an "executive order that will put in place a set of measures designed and aimed against the machinery of apartheid without indiscriminately punishing the people who are victims of that system."[26] The presidential sanctions were, for the most part, similar to those sought by Congress. A key provision dropped from the congressional list by the president was the sanction that mandated a ban on new commercial investment should "significant progress" in dismantling apartheid not be made within twelve months. Most U.S. businesses found that sanction tantamount to disinvestment and strongly opposed it.

The executive order forbade most loans to the RSA, stopped sale of the Krugerrand, banned the sale of computers to all arms of the government that enforce apartheid, and eliminated the export of nuclear technology.[27] While the impact of these sanctions on South Africa is not economically significant, analysts predicted that the South African government would get the message and would make every effort to at least appear responsive. For its part, the Botha administration called the sanctions "a form of warfare" while at the same time reiterating its commitment to overcoming apartheid. Renewed rhetoric about significant upcoming reforms in the pass laws and citizenship for all blacks dominated the media in South Africa.

U.S. Businesses' Involvement in South Africa: The Sullivan Principles

The U.S. corporate presence in South Africa dates back over fifty years. Johnson & Johnson has been there since 1930; General Motors began operations in 1926. Today some 280 U.S. companies operate in South Africa, and they have become embroiled in one of the major controversies of our time. The central issue is whether our corporations should remain in South Africa. Chapter 4 considers the disinvestment question, but first it is important to understand the U.S. business point of view on the matter. Specifically, this section considers the Sullivan Principles, their objectives and their evolution.

One of the most difficult lessons for Americans to learn is that we are not omnipotent in the world, that our influence is quite limited in other societies. This lesson is particularly painful in South Africa where statutory racial discrimination seriously offends our sensibilities, as indeed it should. If it becomes clear that the United States does not have sufficient leverage to overcome the evil of apartheid, then, in my view, it becomes difficult, if not impossible, to justify corporations remaining in that nation. The Sullivan Principles are the chief tool currently employed to exert U.S. influence in the South African society; understanding the scope of this leverage is essential for making a judgment on the ethics of U.S. investments in the land.

Only 4 percent of all the direct investment in South Africa involve foreign multinational companies, and only one-fifth of that investment is from U.S. multinationals. (Direct U.S. involvement is estimated to be about $2 billion.) Thus 0.8 percent of all the investments in South Africa are from U.S. firms. Of all the U.S. monies in direct investment outside the United States, only 1 percent of those funds are invested in South Africa. The typical firm with operations in South Africa has less than 1 percent of total corporate assets in the troubled nation. While today the average rate of return for U.S. investments in South Africa is 5 percent, five years ago it was 31 percent. What this brief financial picture reveals is that the U.S. companies could leave South Africa without an appreciable change in their profits, and that South Africa could probably survive without the U.S. corporate presence.

To be sure, U.S. multinationals presently dominate at least three industries in South Africa: U.S. firms have 30 percent of the automobile industry, 50 percent of the petroleum industry, and 75 percent of South Africa's computer industry. Should the U.S. companies leave South Africa (disinvest), these markets could be readily serviced by other foreign firms, unless, of course, they decided to leave as well. Most believe that there is little evidence that the major trading partners of South Africa—Japan, United Kingdom,

West Germany, Israel, and so on—would join the United States should it decide to disinvest as a sanction to overcome apartheid.

The Sullivan Principles were founded on the premise that U.S. corporate power could be used to dismantle apartheid. It is interesting to note that in the last year the number of signatory companies has grown by 50 percent. Arthur D. Little, Inc., which rates U.S. multinationals on their Sullivan performance, pegs this number currently at 194 against 118 a year ago—most having signed up in the last three months of 1985. For the first time, two South African companies—Carlton Paper Corporation and Vision Video Enterprises—have become signatories. About 90,000 South Africans work for Sullivan signatories, a little less than 1 percent of the work force in the nation. About 80 percent of these workers are black. However, if the non-U.S. companies who have recently adopted a code similar to the Sullivan principles are counted, almost one million blacks in South Africa enjoy the protection of the code.

Chapter 1 discussed the principles in outline, and the Appendix lists them in detail as promulgated by Leon Sullivan. An important feature of the principles is that they continue to be amplified, thus slowly eroding more and more of the apartheid way of life. Originally when they were formulated in 1977, the principles were confined to overcoming apartheid in the workplace. With the fourth amplification in November 1984, however, the goal has been expanded to include the dismantling of apartheid in the wider society. Up till November 1984 the principles covered such issues as desegregation, minimum wages, trade union rights, equal pay for equal work, the elimination of racial discrimination in pay and benefits, advancing black education, and community development. The new dimension of the principles puts U.S. businesses on the leading edge of social change in South Africa:

- Use influence and support the unrestricted rights of black businesses to locate in the urban areas of the nation.
- Influence other companies in South Africa to follow the standards of equal rights principles.
- Support the freedom of mobility of black workers to seek employment opportunities wherever they exist, and make possible provisions for adequate housing for families of employees within the proximity of workers' employment.

• Support the ending of all apartheid laws.

A recent study by the Investor Responsibility Research Center, a nonpartisan research service for university and foundation endowment officers, compared the labor and public affairs activities of signatory and nonsignatory companies.[28] The results of the inquiry reveal remarkable differences in such areas as wages, training and advancement of blacks, desegregation, and funding for black community projects. Sullivan signatory companies were clearly far more active than nonsignatory companies in all the areas *where they are rated annually* in the Sullivan framework. Since the fourth amplification is now part of the rating scheme, it is reasonable to expect some aggressive lobbying by Sullivan signatories designed to overcome apartheid in the wider society.

The present rating scheme is under the direction of the consulting firm of Arthur D. Little. Each year a signatory firm must submit a report outlining all its activities and expenses incurred implementing the principles. Arthur D. Little audits the report and assigns a company one of three ratings relative to the other companies reporting: "making good progress," "making progress," or "needs to become more active."

Since 1978, Sullivan signatory companies have spent more than $130 million on health care, educational development, and housing for blacks in South Africa. Unquestionably, progress has been made, but there is still a long row to hoe before apartheid is dismantled. Believing that strong external pressure is needed on the South African government before substantive changes such as the pass laws and citizenship are tackled, in May 1985 Sullivan issued a timetable for sanctions: "if apartheid has not, in fact, ended legally and actually as a system within the next 24 months, there should be a total U.S. economic embargo against South Africa, including the withdrawal of all U.S. companies, to be followed, I hope, by other nations."[29] There is no question that the U.S. businesses are now applying pressure on the South African government. In September 1985, Roger Smith, chairman and CEO of the General Motors Corporation, and W. Michael Blumenthal, chairman and CEO of Burroughs Corporation, founded the U.S. Corporate Council on South Africa and within two months eighty of the larger corporations operating in South Africa had joined. The purpose of this new coalition is to coordinate efforts with South African business leaders so that a continuing and effective dialogue about apartheid with the South African government authorities may be realized. The charter of the U.S. Corporate Council clearly threatens to enact disinvestment. Listing the purposes of the council, Point 2 reads as follows:

To communicate directly to the South African authorities at the highest levels the strong opposition of Council members to apartheid, and to maintain a continuing dialogue with these authorities, so as to apprise them of the corporate viewpoint as to changes needed to ensure the future viability of the South African economy and U.S. corporate operations there.[30]

Only the future will tell whether this form of pressure is an effective means of dismantling apartheid. For now, many are convinced that it is the most viable means, given the options.

Opponents of the Sullivan Principles

Before 1985, most morally sensitive investors were satisfied that continued progressive reform was possible in South Africa and that the Sullivan Principles ensure that U.S. firms were actively engaged in overcoming apartheid. With the increased violence, the state of emergency and the poor image of the Botha government in the United States, investors have become less confident in the efficaciousness of the Sullivan Principles. Public pension funds of ten states and over 30 cities now have binding legislation mandating divestiture of the stock of companies with South African operations. Church pension funds are considering total divestment, as are educational endowment funds. Some argue that the primary reason for these divestiture moves is political, not moral. Is this the case? How does one discern the ethics of U.S. investments in South Africa? What is the moral thing to do at the juncture in the history of the troubled nation? Chapter 4 considers the arguments made for and against divestment and analyzes the issue.

NOTES

1. See the "Abridged Text of Speech Delivered by State President P. W. Botha on September 30, 1985." Available from the South African Consulate General, 326 East 48th Street, New York, NY 10017.

2. *Ibid.*, p. 2.

3. *Ibid.*, p. 4.

4. Brian Stuart, "Remove Doubt About Reform Objectives, Says Slabbert," *Citizen* (Johannesburg, South Africa) 16 July 1985, p. 12.

5. "Abridged Text," p. 2.

6. See "Address by Mr. D. J. Louis Nel, Deputy Minister of Information of South Africa on October 16, 1985." Available from the South African Consulate General, 326 East 48th Street, New York, NY 10017.

7. "P. W. Warns of 'Deep Potholes' Ahead," *Citizen* (Johannesburg, South Africa) 13 July 1985, p. 2.

8. Quoted in "Quarterly Trends Monitor, June 1985." This publication of the United States-South Africa Leader Exchange Program, Inc. (USSALEP) is available from USSALEP, P.O. Box 23053, Johannesburg 2044. It provides an analysis of the Freedom Charter (p. 15).

9. "Pretoria Takes Action Against Editor," *New York Times* 9 November 1985, p. 4.

10. Howard Barrell, "The United Democratic Front and National Forum: Their Emergence, Composition and Trends," in *South African Review: vol. two* (Braamfontein, South Africa: Ravan Press, 1984), p. 11.

11. Mangosuthu G[atsha] Buthelezi, "Black Demands." An unpublished paper given at the Business International Conference on South Africa: The Evolving Challenge to International Companies, London, England, June 5, 1985, p. 4.

12. *Ibid.*, p. 5.

13. *Ibid.*, p. 6.

14. "Beyers Naude in Conversation with Alan Paton," *Leadership* 3(4) (Cape Town, South Africa), 1984, p. 85.

15. Ted Botha, "State, Church Polarisation," *Pretoria News*, 28 February 1985, p. 10.

16. Lawrence Schlemmer, *Black Worker Attitudes: Political Options, Capitalism & Investment in South Africa* (Durban, South Africa: University of Natal, 1984), pp. 11–15.

17. Lucy Mvubelo, "Foreword," in Richard E. Sincere, Jr., *The Politics of Sentiment* (Washington, D.C.: Ethics and Public Policy Center, 1984), p. ix.

18. "South Africa May Ask Debt Rescheduling in Bid to Halt Mounting Financial Crisis," *The Wall Street Journal*, August 30, 1985, p. 12.

19. "Reform the 'only hope' for South Africa," *Cape Times*, July 31, 1985, p. 9.

20. Hugh Murray, "A Moment in History," *Leadership* 4(3) (Cape Town, South Africa), 1985, p. 30.

21. See David Hauck, Meg Voorhes, and Glenn Goldberg, *Two Decades of Debate: The Controversy Over U.S. Companies in South Africa* (Washington, D.C.: Investor Responsibility Research Center, 1983).

22. For an argument that the United States could do without the "critical materials" imported from South Africa, see Joel P. Clark and Frank R. Field, III, "How

Critical Are Critical Materials?'' *Technology Review*, 88(6) August-September 1985, pp. 38–46.

23. Chester A. Crocker, ''South Africa: Strategy for Change,'' *Foreign Affairs* 59 (Winter) 1980–1981, 323–351.

24. Ronald Reagan, ''South Africa: Presidential Actions,'' Current Policy No. 735. (September 1985) Published by the U.S. Department of State, Washington, D.C., p. 1.

25. Vin Weber and 34 House Republicans to B. G. Fourie, 4 December, 1984. Available from Congressman Vin Weber, U.S. House of Representatives, Washington, D.C. 20515.

26. *Ibid.*, p. 2.

27. *Ibid.*, pp. 2–4.

28. *Recent Developments in Labor Practices in South Africa* (Washington, D.C.: Investor Responsibility Research Center, 1982).

29. Leon H. Sullivan, ''A Deadline for Ending Apartheid,'' *Philadelphia Inquirer*, 7 May 1985, p. 25.

30. Roger B. Smith and W. Michael Blumenthal to Sullivan Signatory Companies, 20 September 1985. Available from Roger B. Smith, Chairman and CEO, General Motors Corporation, Detroit, Michigan 48202.

Chapter 4

U.S. INVESTMENTS IN SOUTH AFRICA: A CHRISTIAN MORAL RESPONSE

For he shall rescue the poor man when he cries out,
  and the afflicted when he has no one to help him.
He shall have pity for the lowly and the poor;
  and lives of the poor he shall save.

Ps. 72(71):12–13

Individual stockholders as well as trustees of institutions are being called on to take a stand on the question of investments in South Africa. For people and institutions who are avowedly Christian, the issue is more pressing. How does one translate the biblical injunction "to love one's neighbor" into this difficult and complex arena? This challenge is the focus in this final chapter. It may appear that I have taken an unnecessarily long route to address the simple question of how a Christian might respond to investing in South Africa, but the earlier chapters are in fact essential. In order to make an ethical judgment about the appropriateness of investments in South Africa, one must first have some knowledge of the situation as it is viewed by black South Africans, as well as a history of the problem and the present alternative strategies proposed for its resolution.

After setting the context in the first three chapters, this chapter offers a Christian theological and ethical approach to the evil of apartheid. Then the various positions advanced for and against disinvestment are considered in light of the theology. Finally, I argue for the position on investments I judge best at this historical juncture. The position argued here is both faithful to the Christian tradition and likely to lead to black liberation.

Theology and Ethics

This past summer I was touring South Africa, researching the ethics of U.S. investments there. After nearly four weeks of traveling throughout the country and interviewing almost a hundred religious leaders, labor leaders, business executives, members of Parliament, and workers, I was left with little hope that South Africa would soon be a peaceful land. About that time I had an interview with Bishop Desmond Tutu. As I walked into his office in Johannesburg, he greeted me exuberantly. My first question was to ask him how he kept so hopeful in the midst of such oppression and violence.

He said, "Let's pray before we talk." We prayed together for several minutes. His prayer called to mind that Jesus Christ came face-to-face with evil, suffered death at its hands, and finally rose again, overcoming evil once and for all. As followers of Christ, we believe that that same pattern can be repeated in each of our lives. Bishop Tutu's challenge is not unlike the challenge that we face: all of us, in our own way, and in our own circumstances, are challenged to overcome evil with good.

The dilemma for the Christian faced with a decision on the ethics of investments in South Africa is that a plethora of responses is offered, each arguing that its perspective is the true one. Thus it is not enough to acknowledge that apartheid is evil and that it must be overcome with good. What does this mean? What constitutes the "good" response to this evil? We all must think this question through for ourselves.

H. Richard Niebuhr, in *Christ and Culture*, expressed in 1951 the problem that many people face today. "So many voices are heard, so many confident but diverse assertions about the Christian answer to the social problem are being made, so many issues are raised, that bewilderment and uncertainty beset many Christians."[1] Niebuhr, after an analysis of the history of Christianity, argues that it may be a foolish endeavor to seek *the* Christian answer to a social problem. Somehow God's plan is to be fulfilled through each arguing for and living out his or her insight into the matter. We all must live our truth, partial though it be; what remains is up to the Lord.

It is helpful also to recall that the repeated struggles of Christians with this problem have yielded no single Christian answer, but only a series of typical answers which together, for faith, represent phases of the strategy of the militant church in the world. That strategy, however, being in the mind of the Captain rather than of any lieutenants, is not under the control of the latter.[2]

After surveying the many ethical arguments made for and against investments in South Africa today, I see three main approaches: (1) the "clean hands" approach, (2) the "solidarity with victims" or prophetic approach, and (3) the "stewardship" approach. Each style has a unique dominant concern. Advocates of the clean hands approach are mainly concerned to avoid complicity in the evil of apartheid. Followers of the prophetic style emphasize the crucial need to identify with the oppressed of South Africa in a clear and dramatic manner, while followers of the stewardship approach seek to determine the best way to use corporate and government power to advance the welfare of black South Africans. Most often those arguing in the "clean hands" and prophetic modes are strong advocates of disinvestment, while the followers of the stewardship ethic argue the case for continuing investment. What guidance does a Christian find in the Bible and in the Church to formulate an ethical stance? Which of the three positions is *the* Christian position? Although I will argue for one of the stances, I contend that all three approaches are appropriate expressions of Christian faith. One's unique vocation as a Christian often determines one's ethical stance.

The "Clean Hands" Approach

Scriptural support can be provided for the three sorts of ethics presented. For example, the "clean hands" approach might rely on those texts stressing that human responsibility for this world is always subordinate to trust in God, who is the final creator of history:

But you, you must not set your hearts on things to eat and drink; nor must you worry. It is the pagans of this world who set their hearts on all these things. Your Father well knows you need them. No; set your hearts on his

Kingdom, and all these other things will be given you as well (Matt. 6:31–33).

The first letter to the Thessalonians offers guidance:

Never try to suppress the Spirit . . . ; think before you do anything—hold on to what is good and avoid *every* form of *evil* (1 Thess. 5:19–22).

Apartheid, as a statutory system that bestows rights on the basis of color and race, is a denial of the fundamental Christian value of human dignity that follows from the conviction that all people are created in the image of God. It is, without a doubt, an evil system, and many would argue that as such it should not enjoy the cooperation of Christians in any shape or form. The Christian is presented with an urgent and radical demand to express the selfless love of Jesus and say no to any cooperation. John Howard Yoder makes a persuasive case that Jesus offers us *the strategy* to pursue the Kingdom of God ''in rejecting the crown and accepting the cross. . . . Jesus thereby excluded any normative concern for any capacity to make sure that things would turn out right.''[3]

In this view, then, the claim on conscience to avoid evil may take precedence over the claim to fashion political and economic strategies to promote justice where these strategies entail cooperation with institutions involved with evil. Until apartheid is dismantled, economic and political cooperation is censored, according to some. Disinvestment is *the* answer. The problem many have noted with this solution, however, is that it fails to help those most in need, those suffering under apartheid. Some have adopted a partial version of this ethic by selectively divesting stock of those companies in South Africa who will not sign the Sullivan Principles, their understanding being that the principles enable one to avoid complicity with apartheid and yet also advance justice. This understanding would, of course, be highly questionable with prodisinvestment groups.

The Prophetic Approach

People who espouse the second model primarily want to make a prophetic statement so that men and women of compassion will join ranks and show solidarity with the oppressed of South Africa. This ethic generally calls for disinvestment and strong economic and trade sanctions. It draws on the biblical witness that we are all one people and are called to express our solidarity with those in special need:

Happy the man who cares for the poor and the weak: If disaster strikes, Yahweh will come to his help (Ps. 41:1).

Matthew Lamb in *Solidarity with Victims* summarizes the central tenet of this stance:

Vox victimarum Vox Dei. The cries of the victims are the voice of God. To the extent that those cries are not heard above the din of our political, cultural, economic, social, and ecclesial celebrations or bickerings, we have already begun a descent into hell. "For I was hungry and you gave me no food. I was thirsty and you gave me no drink. I was a stranger and you did not welcome me, naked and you did not clothe me, sick and in prison and you did not visit me" (Matt. 24:42f.).[4]

The weakness of this approach is that it assumes that this is the unique moment of crisis in South Africa, when an overwhelming show of solidarity will mobilize widespread support. Yet should the broad coalition of resistance not materialize, the oppressed blacks may be even more demoralized. Also for those concerned with overcoming apartheid, it is still unclear how apartheid will be dismantled with this ethic.

The Stewardship Approach

The third type assumes that a Christian ethic is an attempt to spell out a way of living "between the times"; that is, in the period between the time of the resurrection of Christ when the reign of God's justice was inaugurated and the time of the eschatological fulfillment of the Kingdom of God. From the words and deeds, indeed the person of Jesus, we know what we hope for in the coming Kingdom and we actively try to change the world so that the values of justice and peace are a reality, if only a dim one here and now.

The paschal mystery—the crucifixion and resurrection of Jesus

Christ—enables Christians to actively pursue justice, peace, and liberty. It also provides a model of the sort of conflict and struggle entailed in seeking the values of God's Kingdom. God's intentions for all creation have been thwarted by selfishness and pride. Just as Jesus encountered the sin of the world that led to his death, so too Christians should expect to participate in this struggle and self-sacrifice as they attempt to pursue God's intentions in fashioning a world where human dignity is central and is protected by the full range of human rights.

The stewardship approach assumes that no one way of life or ethical stance can embody all the fullness of the anticipated Kingdom of God. Justice (including all that it entails in the way of political and economic rights), nonviolence, solidarity, self-sacrifice, and freedom are all crucial to the anticipated Kingdom. However, various Christian communities and individual Christians will accent some values of the Kingdom and mute others as they struggle to give witness to and further the Lord's vision. From this perspective, the three styles of doing ethics each synthesize a particular aspect of Christian hope with a version of political wisdom. For example, the "clean hands" approach would interpret the victory of Christ over sin and death to mean that through the resurrection of Christ his followers now have the grace to imitate Christ the suffering servant. Pacifists, for example, would focus on this interpretation and give witness to the nonviolence of Jesus.

The third model, however, sees the victory of Christ in the resurrection as the call for Christians to work for justice, even in the face of evil, with the knowledge that God will finally crown their meager successes with his final Kingdom. In this view, the primary challenge is not so much to avoid evil as to do good, even and especially where achieving good is marked by ambiguity and conflict. The traditional "just war" theory is based on this sort of understanding of the paschal mystery.[5] To be sure, the just war theory does not countenance unmeasured force or violence to achieve good, but it does acknowledge that sometimes justice can only be secured in this world by "getting one's hands dirty," and it offers criteria for judging when these exceptions are the case.

The theological underpinnings of this third model differ from the other two models in that in a more comprehensive biblical witness is assumed. While the aversion to evil exhibited in the life of Jesus is central, we also need to attend to our sinful situation and the vocation to advance the reign of justice. To say our situation is sinful is to say that sometimes no choice exists without a regrettable aspect. Rather than absolutize the need to avoid evil, this approach attempts a synthesis with the demand to achieve some semblance of justice in a sinful world. For example, this approach takes very seriously the Gospel of Luke, which shows Jesus beginning his ministry in Galilee by quoting the demands of justice from the book of the prophet Isaiah:

> The spirit of the Lord has been given to me,
> for he has anointed me.
> He has sent me to bring the good news to the poor,
> to proclaim liberty to captives
> and to the blind new sight,
> to set the downtrodden free,
> to proclaim the Lord's year of favor (Luke 4:18–19).

This approach also incorporates the Pauline exhortation that the Christian task is to pursue the good in the face of evil.

> Resist evil and conquer it with good (Rom. 12:21).

In the quest for justice in personal and communal life, this ethic acknowledges that often one is faced with choices, all of which have a regrettable aspect. Although U.S. corporate presence in South Africa may indirectly support an apartheid regime by paying taxes, that presence may at the same time be a constructive force to dismantle apartheid, and the lack of that presence may have dire consequences for many who depend on it for their livelihood. In this account the U.S. corporate presence is moral, even though it may involve cooperation with evil, for that presence is actually creating the conditions to end apartheid.[6] In technical language, the "directly voluntary" consequence, achieving the good, occurs while reluctantly allowing an "indirectly voluntary" consequence, an evil. The judgment is made that there is a proportionately grave reason for permitting the evil affect to occur.

The stewardship model is particularly well suited for managers of public and private institutions. Those charged with stewardship of the common good are often faced with conflicting obligations that are not resolved by a strict application of general principles but rather require the virtue of prudence. Prudential judgments take into account the uniqueness of the situation. Some scholars point to Jesus as the model prudential decision maker. The Gospel of Mark tells of a situation where Jesus encounters conflicting obligations (Mark 2:23–28; 3:1–6). The Pharisees insisted on strict observance of the Sabbath; general rules proscribed a whole range of activities, including picking corn and healing the infirm. On the other hand, the disciples were hungry and began to pick corn and a man needed healing. Even though it was the Sabbath, Jesus made the prudential judgment that corn might be picked and the infirm healed, for the needs of life were judged in this situation to take priority over the obligations of worship. While still acknowledging the obligation to follow the rules of the Sabbath, Jesus chose to honor another claim of conscience in this situation.

Philosophical Ethics

It may be helpful to compare and contrast the two basic approaches to moral reasoning in philosophical ethics to the three types presented here. Most philosophers distinguish between two fundamental styles of ethical argument: the *teleological* approach, which states that the rightness or wrongness of an action depends on the consequences of that action, and the *deontological* approach, which states that rightness or wrongness is independent of usefulness but rather a function of duty.[7] The basic command of the Christian ethic—to love one's neighbor as oneself—would seem to be clearly calling for an ethics of duty (deontological) rather than a goal-seeking (teleological) approach. The "clean hands" and the solidarity-with-victims styles directly flow from obligations to imitate Christ's concerns to avoid evil and to side with the oppressed. From these perspectives, the stewardship approach may appear to sanction a crass attempt to be effective rather than to be right.

The stewardship ethic as described here, however, is not a pure ethic of consequences but is rather a mixed position. The goal to be sought, the teleological dimension, in this position is the Kingdom of God, yet the Kingdom has been brought to light in the words and deeds, the person of Christ (the deontological dimension). Thus the sort of behavior obligated is indeed an integral part of the sort of goal sought. The dilemma occurs when following Jesus' command to seek a just society may require one to "dirty one's hands." For example, maintaining investments in South Africa that are likely to overcome apartheid in the long run may also temporarily indirectly support an apartheid system in the short run. The important question from this stewardship ethic is not so much "Is this action right or wrong, good or bad?" but rather the prior question "What sort of person am I becoming and what sort of community am I shaping by acting in this way? Is this the sort of person I want to be and the sort of community I want to form?"

Some Examples

Some examples of the best arguments in the debate over investments in South Africa may be helpful. Consider three thoughtful responses that typify the range of options offered. First, a statement of Clifton R. Wharton, Jr., chancellor of the State University of New York and an advocate of removing all U.S. investments from South Africa:

> Finally, there comes a point so incompatible with one's respect for humanity itself that compromises with conscience can no longer be tolerated or rationalized. When a human situation so fundamentally affronts every tenet of human values, a public expression of personal opposition is a moral obligation.[8]

Wharton is not claiming that his stand will make things turn out right in South Africa; rather, he refuses to be an accomplice in the evil of apartheid. To participate in the apartheid system is to be morally culpable and the proper response, in this view, is to dissociate oneself. What I am calling the "clean hands" approach, this style of ethics is employed by many for one issue or another in investment decisions. For example, many would not consider investing in a house of prostitution, no matter how high the return on investment. Most would consider prostitution an evil and therefore consider it a duty to avoid complicity in this sort of enterprise. Nor would many think it wise to buy stock in the firm and then try to reform the business.

Walter Fauntroy, representative of the District of Columbia in the U.S. House of Representatives and pastor of New Bethel Baptist Church in Washington, D.C., takes another tack. Fauntroy, as one of the original founders of the Free South Africa Movement, advocates a total withdrawal of U.S. investment. For Fauntroy, joining the movement and pressing for disinvestment is a moral requirement. However, he is not primarily concerned for "clean hands," as in the model just discussed. Rather, he is making a prophetic statement, hoping that his stance will evoke similar sentiments from others who will join the resistance.

It is a matter of personal salvation. When this warfare of life is over . . . the question will be, when I was hungry did you feed me? When I was thirsty did you give me something to drink? When I was sick and imprisoned in South Africa did you come to see about me? And the Lord's answer to us will be, inasmuch as you didn't join the Free South Africa Movement in 1985 when I was trying to declare good news to 25 million poor exploited people you did it not unto me.[9]

For Fauntroy, after the 1984 elections "the South African issue presented us a clear opportunity to reassemble a coalition of conscience around something with which most people have to agree."[10] To be sure, the Free South Africa Movement has had an impact in the United States; in fact, the *Wall Street Journal* argued that this movement was primarily responsible for raising the public consciousness that caused President Reagan to reverse himself and to impose economic sanctions against South Africa in September 1985.[11] Whether these sanctions or even the stiffer ones advocated by the movement will aid in overcoming apartheid remains to be seen.

A stewardship ethic is exemplified in the writings of Gatsha Buthelezi. Buthelezi has little use for arguments from moral purity or prophetic witness but rather focuses on how corporate power can most effectively advance the welfare of blacks:

To stand on American indignant principles by withdrawing diplomatically and economically from South Africa is a luxury that the vastness of American wealth could afford. But indulgence in that luxury for the sake of purity of conscience, whatever genuine motives produce that conscience, would do no more than demonstrate the moral ineptitude of a great nation in the face of challenges from a remote area of the globe.[12]

To be sure, Buthelezi is not uncritical of U.S. corporations in South Africa; he is always prodding them to be "good stewards" and use their influence more aggressively to dismantle apartheid. Yet he is fighting to keep U.S. corporations and investments in South Africa because he needs their leverage in his struggle to overcome apartheid and he needs jobs for his people.

Leon Sullivan, many institutional shareholders who continue to hold stock in U.S. corporations with operations in South Africa and a number of others argue for the morality of investments in RSA with the stewardship ethic. The reasoning here is that since the business community has lent its active support to the black cause, the dismantling of apartheid has begun, however slowly. In five years more changes had been consummated than in the fifty before: the repeal of the Immorality and Mixed Marriages Act, the recognition of black trade unions to the point that over one million blacks now are union members, the ending of "whites only" job reservation, the repeal of the law forbidding nonracial political parties, the establishment of a franchise for mixed-race and Indians (unsatisfactory as it is), and the granting to blacks the right to hold the deed to their land in black townships. The April 1986 announcement that the pass laws will be repealed holds much promise. More important, U.S. business has been on the forefront of initiatives to abolish existing legislation that continues apartheid. Such matters as urbanization and influx control, housing, removals, migrant labor, black business rights, and citizenship are major items aggressively lobbied for by the business community in South Africa. The centerpiece of this business initiative is that all these matters ought to be negotiated with the acknowledged black leaders of RSA. While advocates of continuing U.S. investment in South Africa understand that the internal pressure of blacks themselves is crucial for dismantling apartheid, they also consider the pressure from the business community as an important aid in the struggle.

The stewardship ethic also argues that an important consequence of large U.S. investments in South Africa is the attention that RSA receives by the U.S. media and other institutions of U.S. society.

For example, higher education in the United States has been involved in a number of programs to contribute to black advancement in South Africa. The New England Board of Higher Education has been involved in a program to raise funds to support scholarships for blacks in top universities in RSA. The Carnegie Corporation, with the presidents of major U.S. universities, is funding and planning a number of cooperative ventures with higher education in South Africa. The U.S. South Africa Education Program (SAEP) has brought 290 black South African students to the United States since 1979 for graduate and undergraduate study. Someday the blacks will be running South Africa, no matter what the Afrikaners say or do; the crucial need now is to provide numbers of blacks the education and training that they will require to have the infrastructure of black managers to administer such a nation. The U.S. corporate presence is presently a major source and catalyst for that education.

It is interesting to note that Clifton R. Wharton, Jr., originally argued from a stewardship ethic that the consequences of the U.S. corporate presence in South Africa—"practicing nondiscrimination" and "providing a progressive example"—morally justified the investments. As stated earlier, however, six years later in 1985, Wharton is an advocate of complete disinvestment. Acknowledging that the new initiatives from the business community might offer a glimmer of hope, Wharton feels compelled to champion economic withdrawal:

> For the small minority of blacks employed by progressive U.S. corporations, there have been some changes for the better. But these gains are overwhelmed by the clear evidence that for the vast majority, things have gotten steadily worse, not better, during the last decade.[13]

To be sure, a serious recession has depressed South Africa, yet in my view, the facts tell quite another story: many are more hopeful that change can and will come than is Wharton (even given his rendition of the facts, it is unclear how disinvestment would yield beneficial results). All of us seem to have a point beyond which we will not go in the use of the stewardship ethic; deciding when the pace of change is too slow is a very personal judgment. Some continue to ask, "Slow, compared to what?" Others reach the breaking point and say, "Here I stand; I can do no other."[14]

The Stewardship Ethic and Disinvestment

The stewardship model stressing effectiveness as the dominant moral criterion is also employed by some advocates of complete disinvestment. For example, for ANC president Oliver Tambo, disinvestment is a necessary complement to the internal struggle to overcome apartheid. Its value is that it will weaken the government. Joe Slovo, chief of staff of the military wing of the ANC, has stated that disinvestment ''could save thousands of lives'' by weakening the government and hence ending the white rule with less violence than might otherwise occur. Disinvestment creates the possibility for the end of white rule with a ''transformation short of an apocalypse.'' While both Buthelezi and Tambo are interested in an ethic that employs corporate power to advance the welfare of the blacks, each has a different assessment of how the goal is likely to be achieved.

An Overview

U.S. businesses operating in South Africa must obviously follow the logic of the business system; that is, to serve the public by producing goods and services while making a return on investment. The unique moral dilemma of a business operating in South Africa, however, is that without wanting to, the business is indirectly supporting the white minority government's apartheid policies. All three ethical stances regard apartheid as evil, and in the Christian tradition the presumption is that evil is to be avoided. In the third model, however, the obligation to avoid the evil is not absolute but is rather a conditional obligation that can be overridden if certain conditions are met. For example, from Buthelezi's and Leon Sullivan's perspective, while working within the apartheid system may involve business in complicity with evil, this business presence *could be* a significant instrument in attaining the basic freedoms and human rights so sadly lacking for blacks in South Africa. In a case where values tragically conflict, as indeed they often do short of the final Kingdom, this model draws on political wisdom; that is, some assessment on the basis of past experience of how the desired state of affairs is likely to be attained. On the level of prudential judgment, then, Oliver Tambo and Gatsha Buthelezi obviously disagree, each having a different view of *how* political and economic rights will eventually be realized. Both would agree that value is not merely something never to be violated but rather something to be actively sought, protected, and promoted. But they have differing insights on how one gets things done in this world, differing accounts of political wisdom. Buthelezi is willing to work within the system and will not resort to violence where wholesale slaughter is likely. Tambo sees no hope in the system and violence as a key means.

The statements of Wharton, Fauntroy, Buthelezi, and Tambo point out that in the face of an evil such as apartheid, there are at least three ways of reasoning about the proper course of action. The dominant concern varies in each of the three ethics: avoidance of complicity, seizing the prophetic moment, and the optimum use of power for human welfare. Although many of the key actors in the South African discussion do not hold positions that fit neatly into one of the three ethics described, most do emphasize one or other of these ethics. Thus Wharton's position would find resonance with many ANC and AZAPO leaders. Fauntroy's stance is similar to many United Democratic Front leaders, and religious leaders such as Byers Naude. Buthelezi's position is mirrored by some South African labor leaders and is also held by Sullivan in the United States. Tambo's approach is shared by some UDF leaders.

Obviously, I am most sympathetic with this third model, which stresses that the dominant moral criterion should be the consequences that advance human welfare; but this is not to say that the other two models are devoid of truth. The strength of the stewardship model is that it unabashedly pursues justice even when this, within limits, requires "dirty hands." The weakness of this approach is that one can get so involved in the intricacies of managing good consequences that one can lose one's moral bearings. Although this approach might allow for cooperation in an apartheid government, for example, it is much too easy to forget that this cooperation is an exception to the rule of avoiding evil. All too often what happens is that the exception, based on some anticipated good consequences (the political rights of blacks), becomes the custom, and the rule promoting the value is neglected. However, if the community is fortunate enough to have a Clifton Wharton or a

Walter Fauntroy, speaking from their respective standpoints, moral bearings are forever rejuvenated. This, to be sure, is no small contribution.

In summary, in my judgment, the synthesis of the biblical witness—Jesus's avoidance of evil, the reality of sin and the vocation to realize justice in the world—and political wisdom enable one to justify U.S. investments in South Africa as moral. This judgment of morality is predicated on the fact that the political and economic welfare of the blacks will be enhanced by socially responsive foreign investment. However, a key assumption in this analysis, and one that is the subject of much debate, revolves around the likely effects of investment or divestiture. If it can be shown, for example, that in the long run disinvestment would help blacks much more than hurt them, then one could argue that disinvestment is the moral policy. The assumption of my argument is that continuing investment in South Africa will be more helpful, both in the long and the short run, *for the least advantaged*. This bit of alleged wisdom requires further discussion.

Disinvestment and Political Change

Those arguing for the "prophetic witness" and "clean hands" approach to moral issues would likely claim that the stewardship approach has the fatal weakness of relying on predictions of future consequences to determine the moral quality of a proposed action. Clearly there is some truth to this contention, although I judge it to be a minor weakness rather than a *fatal* weakness of the model. The burden of anyone making an argument about the supposed outcome of certain uses of corporate power is to spell out how that power will bring about the desired consequences. This explanation, of course, requires some testimony from the business economists and others who analyze the effects of investments on the nations' economies.

Disinvestment Advocates: Diverse Agendas

It will be helpful to consider first the scenarios of those who advocate that all foreign capital leave South Africa—the position known as *disinvestment*. As discussed earlier, some advocates of disinvestment argue from moral purity, and their primary objective is to dissociate themselves from an evil situation. A secondary effect of this moral posture often will be to raise the consciousness of others about the plight of blacks. Others may indeed have this strategy as a primary objective when they take a prophetic stand against investment in an apartheid society. Arguments for disinvestment as an instrument of social change are marshaled with two quite different agendas in mind. From an analysis of their public statements, advocates have two diverse objectives in view: violent overthrow of the present government and reform of the present government.

Disinvestment as an instrument to further violent revolution has as its chief exponent the exiled leadership of the ANC. Oliver Tambo and other leaders see no other resolution except revolutionary violence, and the current strategy is to pursue guerrilla warfare and sabotage. In this view, disinvestment will weaken the white racist rulers and thus hasten the day when the black revolution will triumph. The ANC's mission in exile, broadcasting on 30 July 1985, expressed their plan:

We shall continue bringing the apartheid economy to its knees. Whether the USA and Britain like it or not we shall impose sanctions on our own. Whether they impose sanctions or not their investments in our country shall be placed in jeopardy. There is no way in which these blood suckers can stop us from damaging the machines in the factory. They can't stop us from attacking delivery vans and disrupting communication lines.[15]

The logic of the ANC position is that disinvestment will appreciably weaken the white racist government through weakening the economy and that therefore it is a salutary policy. This argument for disinvestment as an instrument of social change is the major theme of the ANC, though on occasion they have also argued for disinvestment on moral purity grounds. If the economy is appreciably weakened, people will lose their jobs, morale will be lowered, and thus domestic opposition to the government will be heightened. At this same time, the tightened budget will inevitably lower the funds available for the South African military, according to the ANC scenario.

Pacifists, of course, focusing on the nonviolent witness of the

New Testament, would not join ranks with the ANC violent strategy no matter how much economic or political utility were promised.[16] However, many Christians sympathetic to some version of the just war theory could reluctantly allow for revolution if it were clear that legal or peaceful means for resolving the oppression were of no avail.[17] The tough question in this perspective is the one of proportionality: Will the harm caused by an act of revolutionary violence be outweighed by the value that it can reasonably be expected to promote and protect?[18] I, for one, oppose Oliver Tambo and the ANC leadership for resorting to a violent strategy at this stage of the conflict.

Disinvestment as an instrument of political reform has quite another logic. In this scenario, the disinvestment movement serves as a way to pressure the South African government to make reforms and finally to come to the negotiating table. To be sure, some companies will actually have to leave South Africa so that the threat of total disinvestment is a real one, but there is the unspoken assumption that total disinvestment will not be necessary. The rhetoric is often high pitched, but the common conviction of this school is that economic pressure is the "only alternative to armed struggle." Many statements of the UDF, the South African Council of Churches (SACC), and Bishop Desmond Tutu fall in this category. In June 1985, SACC released a statement typical of this stance, calling for economic sanctions, including disinvestment, arguing that these measures serve "as a peaceful and effective means of putting pressure on the South African Government to bring about the fundamental changes this country needs."

Disinvestment threats in this context play a role somewhat analogous to the concept of deterrence in nuclear ethics.[19] According to this doctrine, a threat to use nuclear weapons against an adversary deters that adversary from using military force. Of course, if the policy is effective, the nuclear weapons will never be used. Similarly, if the policy of threatening disinvestment is effective, actual disinvestment need never occur. Again, the proportionality question is the relevant one for formulating a moral judgment on this policy: Will the harm caused by marshaling public opinion for disinvestment be outweighed by the value it can be reasonably expected to promote and protect? Since the South African government seems to have responded to this disinvestment pressure with some reform measures, as indicated in Chapter 1, there is evidence for its effectiveness.

On the other hand, the strident posturing of disinvestment advocates may so raise the opposition of the public in the United States and other RSA trading-partner nations, that the multinational companies may leave South Africa rather than contend with the hassle at home. Without the U.S. corporate presence, the South African blacks will definitely lose much of the extensive U.S. media coverage, no small loss in the campaign to capture international attention for their plight. This is not even to mention the economic power and its accompanying social power that may be forever lost should the disinvestment movement actually succeed. This second issue is discussed later.

Before 1985, it would have been safe to say that most church activists and other concerned people in the United States were advocating disinvestment in South Africa as an "instrument of political change." The primary tactics were shareholder resolutions, active lobbying at corporate annual meetings, and other campaigns designed to raise the consciousness of the public. The actual selling of stock in companies operating in South Africa was relatively rare. During 1985–1986, however, there has been a dramatic shift in approach; many endowment and pension funds opted for divestment. The reasons given for divestment are generally either to make a "prophetic statement" (Model 2), to have "clean hands," or simply to meet the concerns of the relevant constituencies. Over ten states and 30 cities have passed legislation mandating the divestiture of South African-related securities. Some forty educational endowment funds have enacted similar restrictions.

The reasons given for the shift in moral positions are important to note. In September 1985 the Episcopalians approved a divestment program after stating that other activist measures "had not proved effective in promoting change either in the companies or in the South African system."[20] The Episcopal legislative houses indicated that the events in South Africa of the summer of 1985 had changed the climate of opinion.

The State University of New York board of trustees voted to sell all their endowment holdings in companies doing business in South Africa. The trustee sponsoring the resolution, passed in September

1985, offered the following rationale: "Conditions in South Africa have grown more grave, with intensified violence and without significant reform measures having been instituted by the South African government."[21] In October 1985 Columbia University's board of trustees voted to divest. The chairman of the board stated, "we are expressing our abhorrence of apartheid and the South African Government's obdurate adherence to it."[22] In August 1985, New Jersey governor Thomas H. Kean signed a bill that will withdraw pension funds of some $2 billion in investments over a period of three years. In a lengthy statement, Kean made an interesting distinction and gave his rationale for signing the divestment bill:

A university, for example, might argue that its need to protect academic freedom precludes it from using its resources to press its political views on other institutions outside the campus; but that governments have a *duty* to pursue their *ideals*. Harvard University President Derek Bok made this distinction in his 1984 statement on divestment, in which he wrote, "the university is quite unlike other instutitions, such as governmental bodies, which are designed to exert power over others and to be subject in turn to outside pressures from groups seeking to influence the uses of power in a democracy."[23]

Obviously Kean was under tremendous pressure from important segments of his constituency.

What is clear is that a growing number of responsible people are losing confidence that the leverage of U.S. corporate power will overcome apartheid in South Africa. Their objective in divesting fall in two categories: either (1) to avoid complicity in the evil and also to send a signal to the companies that they ought to avoid complicity and leave the troubled nation, or (2) by the publicity of divestiture, to increase the pressure on the South African government in hopes that substantive reform measures will finally be adopted. This latter strategy is a last-ditch effort to employ the disinvestment as an "instrument of political reform model." In many cases the two logics—"complicity" and "instrument of political reform"—are intertwined in the rationales for divesting.

Leverage: How Much Do Foreign Investors Have?

Before examining the likelihood that economic deprivation initiated by disinvestment will lead to political change in South Africa, it is important to review the extent to which economic deprivation can be induced by the departure of foreign investments. As might be expected, the economists are not of one mind on this matter.[24]

There does seem to be a consensus by the experts that while disinvestment would not cripple the South African economy, it would have negative consequences. While there is some debate on the short-term effects, most judge that in the long run the lack of modern technology and advanced managerial skills that accompany multinational financial investment would result in job loss and slower economic growth.[25]

Foreign sources supply only 10 percent of the total investment in South Africa, according to government sources. Although the actual figures are exceedingly difficult to verify, analysts estimate that direct foreign investment is about R20 billion (20 billion rand) and indirect foreign investment (bank loans and stockholdings) is another R20 billion. Fueled by the concern over South Africa's short-term debt and the increasingly visible political unrest, there has been a growing loss of confidence in the rand; the rand declined in exchange value for the dollar by almost a factor of two-thirds from 1984 to 1986. Thus the figure for U.S. dollars invested in South Africa continues to decline even if there is no capital outflow. As indicated in Chapter 3, estimates are that the U.S. share of direct foreign investment is about $2 billion, about 0.8 percent of all direct investment. Estimates vary for bank loans from $3.5 to $4.5 billion.

Most analysts are not convinced that economic sanctions will ever provide sufficient leverage to force political change. This doubt is based both on a historical study of the Afrikaner character (Chapter 2) and careful calculation of foreign economic clout. Many argue that the most potent economic weapon has already been set in motion, the "calling" of payment of the external short-term debt of South Africa. As discussed in Chapter 1, much RSA debt (some $19–22 billion) is largely short term—48 percent of the private sector debt has a six-month maturity while 60 percent has twelve months. The refusal to roll over this debt until some strong signs of political stability are evident turns out to be considerable leverage. It is unclear, however, that it will result in substantive reform.

No matter what, many believe the existing level of foreign investment will remain about the same; should U.S. or other major investors be forced to sell under pressures from home, other foreign corporations will buy most of the assets. In the financial market crisis in August 1985, the government reintroduced the financial rand and a two-tier currency control plan. The financial rands are short-term deposits from the sale of assets in South Africa by nonresidents and must be held in South African banks. The upshot of these controls is that foreign investors can only take capital proceeds out of South Africa as new investors put assets in the nation. Thus, at this time it is difficult to move capital out of South Africa. The real issue, then, is how much new foreign capital will be coming to South Africa. As long as investors know that it will be difficult to remove their funds, the prospect for the infusion of new capital is bleak.

If the U.S. government were to require disinvestment and even trade boycotts, most feel that such moves would not place very much additional pressure on the South African government. The majority of the exports from South Africa are what are called "fungible" goods, such things as coal, corn, diamonds, gold, and platinum, which cannot be identified by country of origin and which are widely sought in the global economy. If the United States boycotted South African exports, most of the goods would come to the United States through middlemen at a higher price. There is little precedent for success in these matters.

The disinvestment scenario requires internal unrest heightened by unemployment and a poor economy as a result of disinvestment. I understand the passion people have to find a quick way to end apartheid, for I feel it myself. After seeing the situation at first hand and after considerable reflection, I do not think that divestiture is an effective means for bringing about the situation envisioned by its advocates who seek political change in South Africa. The only way that the U.S. disinvestment campaign would even have a chance to achieve its desired effect is if the U.S. sanctions were also adopted by the international community. At present Great Britain, West Germany, Japan, Taiwan, and Israel carry on significant commerce in South Africa, and they demonstrate little interest in sanctions. Taiwan alone opened twenty factories in South Africa in the last two years. I met marketing people in South Africa who assured me that Japanese and European computer firms were already telling customers that U.S. firms may leave South Africa and that they should buy their products from non-U.S. sources.

The reasons why our allies will not join in economic sanctions are not as simple as lack of concern for the oppressed blacks. In fact, this is most often not the case. Consider the case of Britain. Seven to ten percent of all Britain's foreign investment is in South Africa; it has twice our stake in South Africa and almost 50 percent of all the foreign investment in the RSA. Estimates are that 250,000 British jobs depend on South African trade; exports from the United Kingdom to the RSA last year amounted to $1.7 billion worth of goods. It has been a long-standing policy of the British government that they could not afford economic sanctions; the domestic economy of the United Kingdom is far from robust as it is. By all accounts, the U.S. could never count on Britain to support any economic sanctions toward South Africa.

Disinvestment by U.S. firms, in my judgment, will not bring about the economic deprivation envisioned by its advocates. With an upper limit of some 100,000 jobs in South Africa and a very modest percent of the total direct investment, the United States does not possess sufficient economic power to make that sort of negative impact. To be sure, the South African economy would be better off *with* U.S. investments, but it could manage without them. While I cannot prove *conclusively* that U.S. disinvestment would not cause the other nations to join the withdrawal, I find little evidence to support that hypothesis. Alan Paton, author of *Cry, the Beloved Country*, and a liberal who has given most of his life to fighting apartheid, recently summed up my position well: "To believe that disinvestment will bring our Government 'to its knees' is to believe nonsense."[26]

Black Attitudes Toward Disinvestment

The most powerful and compelling argument for disinvestment is one that makes the case that this is what the overwhelming majority of black South Africans are asking of the international community. Whether their objective is to punish the white minority government, to increase leverage, or to take a prophetic stand, a positive response by the major trading-partner nations to such a black demand would have an enormous effect on black morale. Blacks would feel supported, and the white government would lose much of its legitimacy in the international and domestic arenas. Whether in fact apartheid would be overcome by such an economic withdrawal is quite another story, and many blacks understand that. Do blacks actually want foreign investments to leave South Africa?

From my interviews in South Africa, when blacks equate disinvestment with economic hardship in their land, they have a mixed response. However, almost all blacks want any help the international community can provide in alleviating their plight. "Use your influence to help us in our struggle for freedom" was almost the unanimous sentiment. A meeting I had one Sunday morning with the parish council of a church in Soweto in many ways was a microcosm of my findings throughout the nation. One person, a middle-aged businessman, argued passionately against U.S. disinvestment; he said many of his friends and neighbors would suffer dire economic hardship, and it was not clear that any good would come of it. Another member, a woman who had raised five children, championed disinvestment as the last hope to avoid a bloodbath; she felt the white government would finally come to the negotiating table with this sort of pressure. As I asked the others present, it was clear that the group was about evenly divided between the two positions.

Empirical research on black attitudes to disinvestment is controversial and of limited value, in my judgment. A 1984 study by Lawrence Schlemmer of the University of Natal of black workers in industrial centers of multinational investment revealed only 25 percent support for disinvestment.[27] Schlemmer's questions, according to critics, so identified disinvestment with loss of jobs, that a fair reading of the issue was not obtained.[28] Market Research Africa, surveying a cross-section of the population, found even less support for disinvestment. Markinor, another research group, in August 1985 polled 400 urban blacks; 77 percent agreed that countries should "impose economic sanctions unless South Africa agrees to get rid of the apartheid system."[29] This study, too, has been the subject of much criticism.

Black trade unions do not have a consensus on disinvestment. Public statements of the Congress of South African Trade Unions (COSATU) and the Council of Unions of South Africa (CUSA) are prodisinvestment, while those of the National Union of Clothing Workers and its parent organization, the Trade Union Council of South Africa (TUCSA) are antidisinvestment. The Black Allied Workers Union (BAWU) and the South African Boilermakers' Society (65 percent nonwhite) have opposed disinvestment.

The UDF, ANC, and AZAPO, to one degree or another and with diverse rationales, support disinvestment. Inkatha opposes disinvestment.

After considering the empirical research, the vast literature and reflecting on my experience in South Africa, the finding of the 1982 Rockefeller Report still seems valid: "Our impression is that blacks who reflect on foreign investment as an issue are roughly divided between those favoring disinvestment and those who would like to see it remain in instances where it contributes to black aspirations directly and in the near term."[30]

Business in South Africa: The Challenge and the Promise

From all my reading and research and from extensive interviews with blacks in South Africa, I clearly see that many blacks do not understand why so many Americans cherish capitalism in a democratic polity. It is only a slight exaggeration to say that the particular amalgam of democracy and capitalism found in South Africa is the most persuasive argument for the Marxist revolutionaries, if only because they offer an alternative to the status quo. Recall Chapter 1 and the suffering of the young black executives; of course, they are in a distinct, relatively affluent minority. A "democracy" controlled by 20 percent of the population who use laws and police to control the other 80 percent is hardly an attractive form of government. "Free enterprise" that perpetuates an economic order where, for the most part, only whites are educated for the good positions and that continues disproportionately to enrich the white minority will have little appeal. Blacks in South Africa who have been trained and given an opportunity to perform in the free-enterprise system sing its praises. Many, however, favor a vague "socialism," which generally means an economic order that respects them as people and offers them a chance for a humane life. What can business and particularly U.S. business do to change these perceptions?

As I have argued, I believe that the moral policy is for U.S. corporations to remain in South Africa and use their influence to dismantle apartheid. The expanded Sullivan Principles offer business a broad challenge to overcome apartheid, but the principles need to be creatively implemented and applied so that blacks clearly perceive that U.S. business is *on their side*. Few would argue that economic growth in itself will provide sufficient leverage to dismantle apartheid, although the rise of black trade unions with their countervailing power is obviously one spinoff of such growth. What business needs today, however, is dramatic new initiatives not only to appease the critics at home but to ensure their future in South Africa. From the moral perspective, where business has power there is also commensurate responsibility to overcome apartheid.[31] Enlightened self-interest will most often support the moral perspective. Business has potentially vast new markets in South Africa if the blacks can be brought into the society as full-fledged citizens with consumer power. For this ever to become a reality, blacks must clearly see that business is their ally in the struggle.

Business must be very straightforward about acknowledging the sort of government currently in power in South Africa. The history of the country (Chapter 2) as well as the public statements of the government (Chapter 3) offer much evidence that the contemporary Afrikaner is torn between a desire to share power while at the same time maintaining control. While the futility of searching for such a formula may be obvious to outsiders and to many South African business executives schooled in pragmatic and rational compromises, it is not nearly so obvious to many Afrikaner politicians accustomed to holding all the power. Business must continue pressing the case for rational compromise by initatives similar to those already undertaken (Chapter 3) and by new and more dramatic moves. Business as an institution must be *clearly* on the side of the blacks.

One of the most powerful but seldom-mentioned arguments for U.S. business remaining in South Africa is that the very presence of extensive U.S. investments there ensures heavy media coverage of societal problems. A friend who worked with the church in Uganda for a number of years lamented that many more blacks have been slaughtered in Uganda and that their plight gets relatively little notice in U.S. newspapers and television. That South Africa appears relatively attractive to the blacks of the African continent is evident by the hundreds of thousands of blacks who each year vote with their feet, crossing the border into South Africa to find employment. Admitting that there are clearly unexpected benefits to a strong business presence in South Africa in no way diminishes the urgency for effective corrective action.

To assume that business alone could reform South African society is to miss the point. Business is only one of the institutions that must assume dramatic new roles. While the subject of this study is the ethics of U.S. investments and hence has a focus on business, the assumption is that if the problem is ever to be resolved, *all* the major actors on the South African scene must intensify their participation, especially the churches, the higher-educational institutions, the foundations, the U.S. government, and the international community.

Several examples of leading U.S. firms in the area of social responsibility may call attention to what is being done and what remains to be done. Any number of firms might qualify for discussion here, including Burroughs, Colgate-Palmolive, Control Data, Eastman Kodak, General Motors, IBM, Mobil, and Texaco. Two firms I had the opportunity to visit in South Africa are worth highlighting; Johnson & Johnson and Coca-Cola. I also had the opportunity to discuss South Africa with top U.S. management of these two firms, and I am confident of their resolve on the issue. Johnson & Johnson has three companies in South Africa with a total of about 1,500 employees. They were one of the first companies to put a black member on their board of directors of the South African operation. Such an appointment may appear to be simply tokenism, but this sort of symbolic move is not *simply* anything, but is rather the kind of activity that, repeated a thousandfold, could restore black dignity. I had the opportunity to talk to one of the current black directors, businessman Eric Mafuna, and found him to be one of the most knoweldgeable and intelligent persons of any race that I met in South Africa.

Johnson & Johnson (J & J) has spent considerable resources preparing blacks for responsible management positions and has a number of black supervisors (some of whom oversee whites). It was one of the first companies to recognize a black trade union, and periodically uses outside industrial relations consultants to listen to the concerns of their workers. The director of human resources for J & J in South Africa was released for a year to serve as the first coordinator of the South African Task Groups implementing the Sullivan Principles.

Educational programs in the community have received considerable support from J & J. For example, the company has "adopted" nine schools, supplying scholarships and needed financial support. Housing programs for employees have been initiated with the company providing the funding and support so that blacks, for the first time, can buy homes.

Finally, J & J has been at the forefront of efforts by the American Chamber of Commerce to initiate forceful dialogue over black rights with the RSA government. A group meeting with a special South African cabinet committee in 1985 set out the agenda for black civil and political rights considered essential for continued operations in the economy. Top management of J & J is involved with the new U.S. Corporate Council on South Africa and is continually reviewing potential strategy to reach the RSA government and the black community.

The Coca-Cola Company has just under 5,000 employees in South Africa. The company has been a very active participant in the same sort of activities as just described. Given the nature of the enterprise, Coke has been able to integrate numbers of blacks into well-paying jobs such as truck drivers, refrigeration repairmen, and so on. In a major new initiative announced in 1986, the Coca-Cola Company began a new South African-based foundation with an initial commitment of $10 million. Called the Equal Opportunity Fund, it will primarily be concerned with supporting black education, housing, and business development. What is really new, for South Africa at least, is that this fund will be under the control of black South Africans, including the Archbishop of Cape Town, Desmond Tutu, and UDF leader Allan Boesak. Recognizing that "economic apartheid" could be almost as bad as political apartheid, the company is making a major thrust toward black business development. These sorts of imaginative programs may save the day in South Africa. In addition, moves to dismantle the oppressive apartheid laws must be accelerated. In early 1986 General Motors announced from their Port Elizabeth headquarters that the firm will pay the legal fees of blacks violating certain apartheid laws. Other firms are considering sponsoring multiracial housing areas. This sort of activity must be much more commonplace.

In my view, as long as blacks perceive that U.S. corporations are interested in advancing the black cause, those corporations will be welcome in South Africa. The moral duty, then, is not to flee but to remain in South Africa and overcome apartheid. Since more than 50 percent of the market share of many U.S. companies in South Africa is in fact catering to blacks, those companies will know by their balance sheet when to leave; the others, should the day come, may have to be told in more direct ways by the U.S. government. For now, I, for one, hope the U.S. corporations will hang in there and not run away from the challenge.

NOTES

1. H. Richard Niebuhr, *Christ and Culture* (New York: Harper & Row, 1951; Torchbook edition, first edition, 1956), pp. 1–2.
2. *Ibid.*, p. 2.
3. John Howard Yoder, *The Politics of Jesus* (Grand Rapids, Mich.: Eerdmans, 1972). p. 240.
4. Matthew L. Lamb, *Solidarity with Victims* (New York: Crossroad, 1982), p. 23.
5. See David Hollenbach, S.J., *Nuclear Ethics: A Christian Moral Argument* (New York: Paulist Press, 1983).
6. For an elaboration of my position on proportionality, see Oliver F. Williams, "Business Ethics: A Trojan Horse," *California Management Review* 24, 1982, 14–24.
7. See William K. Frankena, *Ethics* (Englewood Cliffs, N.J.: Prentice-Hall, 1973).
8. Clifton R. Wharton, Jr., "Economic Sanctions and Their Potential Impact on U.S. Corporate Involvement in South Africa," House of Representatives Committee on Foreign Affairs, Subcommittee on Africa; 99th Congress, 1st Session, January 31, 1985, p. 105.
9. Walter Fauntroy, "Dismantling Apartheid," *Sojourners* (February 1985), p. 17. Obviously the Free South Africa Movement hopes to dismantle apartheid; as I interpret Fauntroy, however, his primary thrust is to demonstrate solidarity with the oppressed.
10. *Ibid.*, p. 15.
11. Joe Davidson and David Ignatius, "Sanctions on South Africa Are Seen as a Victory For Randall Robinson and 1960s-Style Protests," *Wall Street Journal*, 7 October 1985, p. 50.

12. Mangosuthu G[atsha] Buthelezi, "Disinvestment Is Anti-Black," *Wall Street Journal*, 20 February 1985, p. 32.

13. Wharton, p. 50.

14. For an insightful discussion of managerial ethics, see Max Weber, "Politics as a Vocation," *From Max Weber: Essays in Sociology*, eds. and trans., H. H. Gerth and C. Wright Mills (New York: Oxford University Press, 1946), pp. 77–128.

15. Quoted in Mangosutha G[atsha] Buthelezi, "King Shaka Day," p. 15. An unpublished paper given in Umlazi, South Africa, on September 28, 1985. Available from the Center for Ethics and Religious Values in Business, University of Notre Dame, Notre Dame, Indiana 46556.

16. For an exposition of this position, see Dom Helder Camara, *Spiral of Violence*, translated by Della Couling (Denville, N.J.: Dimension Books, 1971).

17. Pope Paul VI argues that "insurrection and rebellion" could be morally legitimate where there is "a case of a clear and long-standing tyranny which violates the basic rights of the human person and which is bound up with serious harm to the common good." *On The Development of Peoples*, para. 31. See Thomas A. Shannon, ed., *War or Peace? The Search for New Answers* (Maryknoll, N.Y.: Orbis Press, 1980); Jon Gunnemann, *The Moral Meaning of Revolution* (New Haven, Conn.: Yale University Press, 1979); and William V. O'Brien, *The Conduct of Just and Limited War* (New York: Praeger, 1981).

18. For an excellent discussion of proportionality, see Richard McCormick and Paul Ramsey, eds., *Doing Evil to Achieve Good: Moral Choice in Conflict Situations* (Chicago: Loyola University Press, 1978).

19. See Richard A. McCormick, "Notes on Moral Theology: 1982," *Theological Studies* 44, 1983, 87–94.

20. "Divestment Plan Approved By Episcopal Church Group," *New York Times*, 13 September 1985, p. 8. The tougher stance is also evident in the position of a new coalition of church groups affiliated with the Interfaith Center on Corporate Responsibility. In the spring of 1985, singling out 12 U.S. corporations who "support the South African government through products and services used by the police and military; the significance of their presence in terms of assets, sales, and number of employees; the strategic nature of their involvement; or through financial services and lending to the South African government," the coalition intends to pressure the firms to leave RSA unless major changes are enacted by Pretoria.

   At its August 1985 meeting, the Lutheran World Federation Executive Committee issued a "Background Paper and Statement on Southern Africa" (Exhibit 20.3), which endorsed the call for economic sanctions issued by the South African Council of Churches. Investments are to be reviewed so that "LWF pension fund investments are not made in companies doing business in South Africa or Namibia" (Article 3.3).

21. "New York State U. Votes Sale of Its South Africa Holdings," *New York Times*, 25 September 1985, p. 9. Clifton R. Wharton, Jr., had argued against divestiture. "Should universities and other institutions divest themselves of stock in companies that remain in South Africa? I do not think so. I continue to believe that stock divestiture is at best a simplistic symbolism that fails to understand the complex interrelationships among firms and their suppliers. . . . Aside from their brief publicity value, divestiture campaigns inflict no 'punishment' on South Africa. While divestiture might salve the egos of those activists who are

indiscriminately against 'big business,' it would have no direct effect on real matters at hand. All that would happen is that somebody else would buy the stock." "Economic Sanctions," pp. 104–105.

22. Robert D. McFadden, "Columbia to Sell Stock Linked to South Africa," *New York Times*, 8 October 1985, p. 1.

23. "Statement of Governor Thomas H. Kean Concerning Divestiture of New Jersey State Pension Funds From Companies Doing Business in South Africa" (Assembly Bill No. 1309), p. 4. Governor Kean asked the Legislature "for the passage of a measure which would give the Governor the authority to modify divestiture based on the future actions of the South African government." This would enable the New Jersey position still to be an "instrument of political reform" while also being "prophetic." The best amalgam of these models is the divestiture program of the New York City Employees Retirement System (NYCERS); that plan allows for a company to avoid divestiture if certain objectives are met within a specified time.

24. The following are helpful in understanding the potential influence of disinvestment on the South African economy: F. Fisher, L. Schlemmer and E. Webster, "Economic Growth and Its Relationship to Social and Political Change," in L. Schlemmer and E. Webster, eds., *Change, Reform and Economic Growth in South Africa* (Johannesburg: Raven Press, 1978); S. Gelb, "Unemployment and the Divestment Debate," *South African Labour Bulletin* 10 (6), 1985; H. Houghton, *The South African Economy* (Cape Town: Oxford University Press, 1976); T. Koenderman, *Sanctions: The Threat to South Africa* (Johannesburg: Jonathan Ball, 1982); G. Muller, "Multinational Companies in South Africa," in J. Matthews, ed., *South Africa in the World Economy* (New York: McGraw-Hill, 1983); D. Myers, D. Propp, D. Hauck, and D. M. Liff, *U.S. Business in South Africa* (Bloomington: Indiana University Press, 1980); A. Spandau, *Economic Boycott Against South Africa: Normative and Factual issues* (Johannesburg: Juta, 1979); H. Strack, *Sanctions: The Case of Rhodesia* (Syracuse, N.Y.: Syracuse University Press, 1978); and N. M. Stultz, "Sanctions, Models of Change and South Africa," *South Africa International* 13 (2), 1982.

25. Some argue that in the short term disinvestment would protect jobs due to a slower rate of technical change. Since some imported technology is capital intensive, the loss of these multinationals would not increase unemployment. This loss would encourage import substitution and be a stimulus to development of local technical expertise. In the long term, however, most argue that disinvestment, while it would not cripple the economy, would result in a misallocation of resources. For a contrary opinion, see J. Davis, J. Cason, and G. Hovey, "Economic Disengagement and South Africa," *Law and Policy in International Business* 15 (2), 1983, 529–63; these authors argue that disinvestment would cripple the economy.

26. Alan Paton, "South Africa Is in a Mess," *New York Times*, 3 April 1985, p. 27.

27. Lawrence Schlemmer, *Black Worker Attitudes: Political Options, Capitalism and Investment in South Africa* (Durban, South Africa: University of Natal, 1984).

28. See M. Sutcliffe and P. Wellings, "Disinvestment and Black Worker 'Attitudes' in South Africa: A Critical Comment," unpublished paper, 1985. The paper is available from M. Sutcliffe, University of Natal. See also the "Rejoinder" by Lawrence Schlemmer, University of Natal.

29. This survey was reported in the *Sunday Star* (Johannesburg) August 25, 1985 and quoted in Jack Brian Bloom, *Black South Africa and the Disinvestment Dilemma: An Exploratory Study of Attitudes Within an Ethical Framework*, a research report for the M.B.A., University of Witwatersrand, September 1985, p. 254.
30. *South Africa: Time Running Out* (Berkeley: University of California Press, 1981), p. 420. This statement is actually a quote from a 1977 study by the U.S. Embassy in South Africa. It is quoted by the Rockefeller Foundation supported "Study Commission on U.S. Policy Towards Southern Africa" as a way of summarizing its findings.
31. The position of the Rev. Leon H. Sullivan is similar to the one argued here: "The Sullivan principles are working. As a result of them, U.S. plants are desegregated, equal pay for equal work is beginning to be paid to black workers, blacks are being elevated to administrative and supervisory jobs, blacks are supervising whites, blacks are being trained with new technical skills, independent free black trade unions are being recognized, schools are being built, housing developments are being constructed, health centers and programs are being initiated, and young blacks by the thousands are being assisted with better education.

   "Also, the impact of the principles goes far beyond these gains, and the opportunities provided the limited number of blacks employed by American companies, who are less than 1 percent of the total black workforce. The principles are a catalyst for change and affect conditions for black workers throughout the country. They are a lever on other companies.

   "A group of South African companies employing a million workers, mostly blacks, are now using the principles in their practices. The principles have started a revolution in industrial race relations across South Africa. Also, they have become a platform for many in South Africa arguing for equal rights in government and other places."

   Sullivan, using the threat of disinvestment, goes on to say that unless apartheid is dismantled by May 1987, there should be "a total U.S. economic embargo against South Africa." *Philadelphia Inquirer*, 7 May 1985, p.A-25.

CONCLUSION

The force of this work has been to argue that U.S. investments in South Africa are indeed moral when it can be shown that these investments are likely to advance the welfare of the blacks, finally yielding the political equality so desperately sought. While acknowledging that apartheid is evil and that U.S. business does unintentionally support the apartheid government by its presence in South Africa, this presence is judged to be moral by the principle of proportionality; that is, that proportionately good consequences are likely to occur. The theology underlying this stance is a synthesis of the biblical witness—the avoidance of evil, the reality of sin and the vocation to realize justice in the world—with political wisdom.

One of the purposes of Chapters 2 and 3 has been to provide some context for making a judgment on the "way the world works" (political wisdom) in that part of the globe. What becomes clear is that the Afrikaners have been blinded to the suffering they were inflicting on the blacks, in part, because of the great suffering their own people had endured in Africa. In their own view, the Afrikaner struggled heroically, against terrible odds and cruel oppressors, in the Anglo-Boer War. Twenty percent of their people, mostly women and children, died in that conflict. They vowed never again to be dominated by another group, and they have singlemindedly kept that vow, even while inflicting a form of violence on the blacks not too unlike the violence the British inflicted on them. The situation has all the makings of a Greek tragedy, and one can only hope that the recent reform measures are the beginnings of genuine insight into the horror of apartheid. The U.S. government must be much more creative in pressing the South African leaders to move ahead with the task of overcoming apartheid. Both U.S. business and government must continue to pressure the South African government to go to the negotiating table with acknowledged black leaders.

While the recent reforms are far from satisfactory and do little to ameliorate Grand Apartheid, it is still true to say that more reform measures have been enacted between 1981 and 1985 than previous governments had done in decades. There has been the repeal of the Immorality and Mixed Marriages Acts, the recognition of black trade unions, the ending of "whites only" job reservations, the repeal of the law forbidding nonracial political parties, the establishment of a franchise for mixed-race persons and Indians (unsatisfactory as it is), and the granting to blacks the right to hold the deed to their land in black townships. The April 1986 announcement that the pass laws will be repealed holds much promise. Obviously, much more needs to be done, but there *are* signs of hope.

Part of the burden of the final chapter is to demonstrate that although the United States and its business firms have only limited influence on what happens in South Africa, that influence ought to be used to advance the welfare of the blacks as effectively as possible. What this might mean for business is some dramatic new initiatives. As far as the U.S. government's position, it was sad to find that almost every black I met in South Africa asked me why my government was so aligned with the white rulers. "Why does the U.S. government not support blacks in their struggle for freedom and democracy?" was a persistent question. The U.S. government must be much more adroit in demonstrating support, even if only symbolic, for the blacks of South Africa. Actions such as sending an official U.S. representative to the mass black burial at Mamelodi in December 1985 speak much louder than words. The young blacks are increasingly anti-American, and this is an extremely serious problem that must be addressed by our most talented statespeople.

The force of the argument here is that there are degrees of evil, and that the evil of apartheid in South Africa is one that can likely be overcome with a skilled use of leverage and an active support of black South Africans. Needless to say, I could not begin to make such an argument for all evils that come to mind; for example, this approach could not be applied to the German regime under Hitler.

Fortunately, we all do not see the world from the same angle of vision. The notion of Christian vocation reminds us that our varying perspectives often complement and complete each other. The good steward as the manager of our public and private institutions surely needs the prophet and those keenly attuned to the dark side of human strategies to help maintain moral bearings. We all need the good steward to fashion a more just and humane world!

THE SULLIVAN PRINCIPLES

Principle 1.

Nonsegregation of the races in all eating, comfort, and work facilities.

Each signatory of the Statement of Principles will proceed immediately to

- Eliminate all vestiges of racial discrimination.
- Remove all race designation signs.
- Desegregate all eating, comfort, and work facilities.

Principle 2.

Equal and fair employment practices for all employees.

Each signatory of the Statement of Principles will proceed immediately to:

- Implement equal and fair terms and conditions of employment.
- Provide nondiscriminatory eligibility for benefit plans.
- Establish an appropriate and comprehensive procedure for handling and resolving individual employee complaints.
- Support the elimination of all industrial racial discriminatory laws that impede the implementation of equal and fair terms and conditions of employment, such as abolition of job reservations, job fragmentation, and apprenticeship restrictions for blacks and other nonwhites.
- Support the elimination of discrimination against the rights of blacks to form or belong to government registered and unregistered unions and acknowledge generally the rights of blacks to form their own unions or be represented by trade unions which already exist.

- Secure rights of black workers to the freedom of association and assure protection against victimization while pursuing and after attaining these rights.
- Involve black workers or their representatives in the development of programs that address their educational and other needs and those of their dependents and the local community.

Principle 3.

Equal pay for all employees doing equal or comparable work for the same period of time.

Each signatory of the Statement of Principles will proceed immediately to

- Design and implement a wage and salary administration plan that is applied equally to all employees, regardless of race, who are performing equal or comparable work.
- Ensure an equitable system of job classifications, including a review of the distinction between hourly and salaried classifications.
- Determine the extent upgrading of personnel and/or jobs in the upper echelons is needed, and accordingly implement programs to accomplish this objective in representative numbers, ensuring the employment of blacks and other nonwhites at all levels of company operations.
- Assign equitable wage and salary ranges, the minimum of these to be well above the appropriate local minimum economic living level.

Principle 4.

Initiation of and development of training programs that will prepare, in substantial numbers, blacks and other nonwhites for supervisory, administrative, clerical, and technical jobs.

Each signatory of the Statement of Principles will proceed immediately to

- Determine employee training needs and capabilities, and identify employees with potential for further advancement.
- Take advantage of existing outside training resources and activities, such as exchange programs, technical colleges, and similar institutions or programs.

- Support the development of outside training facilities, individually or collectively—including technical centers, professional training exposure, correspondence and extension courses, as appropriate, for extensive training outreach.
- Initiate and expand inside training programs and facilities.

Principle 5.

Increasing the number of blacks and other nonwhites in management and supervisory positions.

Each signatory of the Statement of Principles will proceed immediately to

- Identify, actively recruit, train, and develop a sufficient and significant number of blacks and other nonwhites to assure that as quickly as possible there will be appropriate representation of blacks and other nonwhites in the management group of each company at all levels of operation.
- Establish management development programs for blacks and other nonwhites, as needed, and improve existing programs and facilities for developing management skills of blacks and other nonwhites.
- Identify and channel high-management-potential blacks and other nonwhite employees into management development programs.

Principle 6.

Improving the quality of employees' lives outside the work environment in such areas as housing, transportation, schooling, recreation, and health facilities.

Each signatory of the Statement of Principles will proceed immediately to

- Evaluate existing and/or develop programs, as appropriate, to address the specific needs of black and other nonwhite employees in the areas of housing, health care, transportation, and recreation.
- Evaluate methods for utilizing existing, expanded, or newly established in-house medical facilities or other medical programs to improve medical care for all nonwhites and their dependents.
- Participate in the development of programs that address the

educational needs of employees, their dependents, and the local community. Both individual and collective programs should be considered, in addition to technical education, including such activities as literacy education, business training, direct assistance to local schools, contributions, and scholarships.

- Support changes in influx control laws to provide for the right of black migrant workers to normal family life.
- Increase utilization of and assist in the development of black and other nonwhite-owned and -operated business enterprises including distributors, suppliers of goods and services, and manufacturers.

Increased Dimensions of Activities Outside the Workplace

- Use influence and support the unrestricted rights of black businesses to locate in the urban areas of the nation.
- Influence other companies in South Africa to follow the standards of equal rights principles.
- Support the freedom of mobility of black workers to seek employment opportunities wherever they exist, and make possible provisions for adequate housing for families of employees within the proximity of workers' employment.
- Support the ending of all apartheid laws.

With all the foregoing in mind, it is the objective of the companies to involve and assist in the education and training of large and telling numbers of blacks and other nonwhites as quickly as possible. The ultimate impact of this effort is intended to be of massive proportion, reaching millions.

Periodic Reporting

The signatory companies of the Statement of Principles will proceed immediately to

- Report progress on an annual basis to Reverend Sullivan through the independent administrative unit he has established.

- Have all areas specified by Reverend Sullivan audited by a certified public accounting firm.
- Inform all employees of the company's annual periodic report rating and invite their input on ways to improve the rating.

INDEX